MONARCHS
OF
SCOTLAND

MONARCHS OF SCOTLAND

by

STEWART ROSS

LOCHAR PUBLISHING

For my mother
in memory of the Scots in her life
A.E.W.H. and G.S.R.

© Stewart Ross, 1990
Published by Lochar Publishing Ltd
No 8, The Holm
MOFFAT
DG10 9JU

British Library Cataloguing in Publication Data
Ross, Stewart
Monarchs of Scotland
1. Scotland. Monarchs, history
I. Title
941.1.00992
ISBN 0-948403-22-5
(ISBN 0-948403-38-1 pbk)
Typeset by Annandale Press Services, Moffat, in 10 on 12pt Palatino.
Printed by Eagle Press plc., Blantyre.

CONTENTS

SUGGESTED FURTHER READING

The best general history of Scotland is the Edinburgh History of Scotland, four volumes (Duncan, A. M., Nicholson, R., Donaldson, G., and Ferguson, W.), recently reprinted by the Mercat Press, Edinburgh, 1987. A second modern multi-volume history is Wormald, J., ed., The New History of Scotland, eight volumes, 1981-4. Other useful works are:

Anderson, Peter D., Robert Stewart: Earl of Orkney, Lord of Shetland 1533-1593, Edinburgh: John Donald Publishers.

Ashley, M., Charles II, 1971.

Balfour-Melville, E.W.M., James I, King of Scots, 1936.

Barrow, G.W.S., Kingship and Unity: Scotland 1000-1306, Toronto; Buffalo: University of Toronto Press, 1981.

Baxter, S.B,. William III and II, 1966.

Bingham, Caroline., James VI of Scotland, 1979.

Bingham, Caroline., James V: King of Scots. 1512-1542, London: Collins, 1971.

Bingham, Caroline., The Kings and Queens of Scotland, 1976.

Bingham, Caroline., Land of the Scots: A Short History, London: Fontana Paperbacks, 1983.

Bingham, Madeleine., Baroness Clanmorris, Scotland Under Mary Stuart: An Account of Everyday Life, London: Allen and Unwin, 1971.

Bourne, Ruth., Queen Anne's Navy in the West Indies, New Haven: Yale University Press, 1939.

Brgger, Anton Wilheim., Ancient Emigrants, A History of the Norse Settlements of Scotland, Oxford: The Clarendon Press, 1929.

Brown, Jennifer, M., Scottish Society in the Fifteenth Centry, New York: St. Martin's Press, 1977.

Buchanan, George., 1506-1582. The History of Scotland, London: Printed by E. Jones, for A., Churchil, 1690.

Buchanan, Patricia Hill., Margaret Tudor, Queen of Scots, Edinburgh: Scottish Academic Press, 1985.

Cariton, C., Charles I, 1981.

Chadwick, N., The Celts, 1986.

Crawford, Osbert Guy Stanhope., Topography of Roman Scotland, North of the Antonine Wall, Cambridge: Cambridge University Press, 1949.

Cruickshanks, Eveline., The Jacobite Challenge, Edinburgh: J., Donald, 1988.

Cunliffe, Barry W., The Celtic World, London: Bodley Head, 1979.

Curle, James., A Roman Frontier Post and Its People, the Fort of Newstead, Glasgow: J., Maclehose and sons, 1911.

Daiches, David., Charles Edward Stuart: the Life and Times of Bonnie Prince Charlie, London: Thames and Hudson, 1973.

Davies, I., The Black Douglas., London: Routledge and K. Paul, 1974.

Delaney, F., The Celts, 1986.

Donaldson, Gordon., All the Queen's Men: Power and Politics in Mary Stewart's Scotland, New York: St. Martin's Press, 1983.

Donaldson, Gordon., Scottish Kings, London: Batsford, 1967.

Donaldson, G and Morpeth, R.S., A Dictionary of Scottish History, 1977.

Douglas, Hugh., Charles Edward Stuart: The Man. The King. The Legend, London: R., Hale, 1975.

Duke, Winifred., The Rash Adventurer: Being An Account, Compiled From Contemporary Records, of Prince Charles Edward Stuart's Expedition into England During The Last Months of The Year, London: Hale, 1952.

Duncan, Archibald Alexander McBeth., Scotland, The Making of the Kingdom, New York: Barnes and Noble, 1975.

Fergusson, J., Alexander the Third, King of Scotland, 1937.

Forester, M., The Rash Adventurer: The Rise and Fall of Charles Edward Stuart, 1973.

Fothergill, Brian., The Cardinal King., London: Faber and Faber, 1958.

Fraser, Antonia., Mary Queen of Scots, London: Weidenfeld and Nicolson, 1969.

Graham, Frank., Hadrian's Wall in the Days of the Romans, Newcastle Upon Tyne: F., Graham, 1984.

Green, Vivian Hubert Howard., The Hanoverians. 1714-1815, New York: Longmans, 1948.

Gregg, Edward., Queen-Anne, London; Boston: Routledge and Kegan Paul, 1980.

Gregg, Edward., Jacobitism, 1988.

Gregg, P., King Charles I, 1981.

Henderson, Isabel., The Picts, New York: Fraeger, 1967.

Henderson, Thomas Finlayson., Mary, Queen of Scots, Her Environment and Tragedy, New York: Charles Soribner's Sons, 1905.

Hewitt, George R., Scotland Under Morton, 1572-80, Edinburgh: J., Donald, 1982.

Hont, Istvan and Ignatieff, Michael, eds., The Shaping of Political Economy in the Scottish Enlightenment, Cambridge: The Cambridge University Press, 1983.

Kenyon, John Philipps., The Stuarts: A Study In English Kingship, London: Fontana, 1970.

Lenman, Bruce., The Jacobite Cause, 1986.

Lenman, Bruce., The Jacobite Risings in Britain, 1689-1746, London: Eyre Methuen, 1980.

Lynch, Michael., Mary Stewart, Queen in Three Kingdoms, New York: B., Blackwell, 1988.

Macdougall, Norman., James III, A Political Study, Edinburgh: J., Donald, 1982.

MacKenzie, Agnes Mure., The Scotland of Queen Mary and the Religious Wars 1513-1638, London: Alexander Maclehose and Co., 1936.

Mackie, John Duncan., A History of Scotland, Baltimore: Penguin Books, 1964.

Mackie, R.L., James IV of Scotland, 1956.

Macquarrie, Alan., Scotland and the Crusades, 1095-1560, Edinburgh: J., Donald Publishers Ltd., 1985.

Marshall, Rosalind Kay., Mary of Guise, London: Collins, 1977.

Mathew, David., Scotland Under Charles I, London: Eyre and Spottiswoode, 1955.

McKelvey, James Lee., George III and Lord Bute: The Leicester House Years, Durham, C.C.: Duke University Press, 1973.

McLynn, F.J., Charles Edward Stuart: A Tragedy in Many Acts, New York: Routledge, 1988.

Millar, P., James [The Old Pretender], 1971.

Miller, J., James II, 1978.

Mitchison, Rosalind., A History of Scotland, London: Methuen, 1970.

New York Public Library, A List of Works Relating to Scotland, New York: The New York Public Library, 1916.

Orel, H. and Snyder. H.L. and Stokstad, M., eds, The Scottish World, 1981.

Pinkham, Lucile., William III and The Respectable Revolution: the Part Played by William of Orange in the Revolution of 1688, Cambridge, Mass.: Harvard University Press, 1954.

Plowden, Alison., Elizabeth Tudor and Mary Stewart — Two Queens in One Isle, Totowa, N.J.: Barnes and Noble Books, 1984.

Plowden, Alison., Two Queens in One Isle: the Deadly Relationship of Elizabeth I and Mary Queen of Scots, Brighton, Sussex: Harvester Press, 1984.

Prebble, John., Glencoe: the Story of the Massacre, New York: Hoit Rinehart and Winston, 1966.

Scott, Ronald McNair., Robert the Bruce: King of Scots, London: Hutchinson, 1982.

Somerset Fry, Fiona and Plantagenet., The History of Scotland, London: Routledge, 1982.

Steel, T., Scotland's Story, 1984.

Szechi, D., Jacobitism and Tory Politics, 1710-14, Edinburgh: J., Donald, 1984.

Terry, Charles Sanford., The Jacobites and the Union, Cambridge: Cambridge University Press, 1922.

Tranter, Nigel G, Land of the Scots, New York: Weybright and Tailey, 1966.

Vaugham, Worbort M., The Last of the Royal Stuarts, London: Methuen and Co., 1906.

Willson, D.H., King James VI and I, 1956.

Wormald, Jenny., "The House of Stewart and its Realm." History Today, Vol.34, 1984.

Wormald, Jenny., Mary Queen of Scots: A Study in Failure, London: G., Philip, 1988.

ACKNOWLEDGEMENTS

This book could not have been assembled in the time that it has without the inspiration and assistance of many people. The author would like to express sincere thanks to the following: members of the Ross family, past and present, for keeping alive the spirit of Scotland; Frances Kelly, for professional advice and guidance; Moria Campbell of the Scottish Tourist Board, Ian O'Riordan and David Patterson of the Edinburgh City Art Centre, Michael Jenner, Deborah Pownall, Alastair Brodie of the National Library of Scotland, Alison Sheridan of the Royal Museum of Scotland, Ian R. Douglas of the Dunecht Estates, Sue Bowland of J. Arthur Dixon, Christine Hall of the British Library, F. W. Manders of Newcastle City Central Library, Judith Prendergast of the National Portrait Gallery, Ian Hill of the Scottish Record Office and Deborah Hunter of the National Galleries of Scotland for their help with illustrations; Caroline Bingham for invaluable help with pictures and other encouragement; Hubert Pragnell for producing the fine maps and family trees from indecipherable originals; Jim and Liz Woodrow of the Peel Hotel, Edinburgh for finding a pleasant room with a table in it; Graeme and Irma for providing pertinent comments from the general reader; Francis and Liz for bed and board; James, Kate, Alexander and Eleanor for putting up with a part-time dad; Marjorie Henderson for providing a peaceful refuge; and, above all, Lucy for typing of the highest standard, invaluable observations and patience way beyond the call of duty.

Picture Credits

Maps by David Langworth, Family Trees by Bob McEwan. Photographs reproduced with the kind permission of the following:

The Scottish Tourist Board; Michael Jenner; National Galleries of Scotland; National Museums of Scotland; J Arthur Dixon; Newcastle City Libraries; National Library of Scotland; Corpus Christi College; National Portrait Gallery; The British Library; Dunecht Estates, The Hon CA Pearson; City of Edinburgh Museums and Art Galleries; Warwick County Record Office; Osterreichische Nationalbibliothek; Woodmansterne Picture Library; Scottish Record Office; Sir David Ogilvy Bart; His Grace the Duke of Roxburghe

INTRODUCTION

This is not a story of great men. Or even of great men and women. Rather, it is an examination of how ordinary people coped when quite extraordinary demands were made upon them. More than any other human being, a monarch has greatness thrust upon him. He has little choice in the matter. It must be admitted that this was slightly less true of the earlier Scottish monarchs than of those who came into their inheritance through primogeniture. Between the 9th and 12th centuries an ambitious member of the royal family could put in a bid for the throne with some prospect of success and without incurring the sort of disapprobation which haunted later regicides and usurpers, and which we find so powerfully evoked in Shakespeare's Macbeth, Richard III, or Henry IV. There was, therefore, an element of limited natural selection about the appointment of a monarch in early medieval times. This helps to explain why in a brutal and unsentimental age so many of them were ruthless, unattractive personalities. Nevertheless, most of the rulers with whom we are concerned in these pages were trapped by the circumstances into which they were born, and they had to make the best they could of them. Some, like Robert III, were just not up to the inherited task. Yet a surprising number, considering the random method of their selection, proved dedicated and able rulers. Until the very end of our period, when Scotland shared her crown with England, a king or queen was the very pivot of government. He — and this is no sexist pronoun, for we are dealing with an almost exclusively male-dominated institution — was expected to be the nation's leading politician, economist, soldier and administrator. To a very real extent the fate of the nation rested in his hands. Thus the history of Scotland's monarchs is very much a political history of the country. A weak or immature monarch invariably meant civil disorder and economic dislocation; a competent hand at the helm ensured respect for law and order, and developments in government which were generally beneficial to the majority of citizens.

Scotland did not emerge according to some divinely appointed plan. In altered circumstances north Britain might have become part of an Irish, Norse or English kingdom. The Highlands were sufficiently different to have formed a state of their own; and a 'middle kingdom' between it and Anglo-Norman England could have been carved out by a vigorous dynasty based in York or Edinburgh. That the nation emerged as it did, stretching from the Shetlands to the Tees, was largely due to the efforts of Scotland's monarchs. Few of them were heroes; some were downright scoundrels. But fired by vanity, ambition and, occasionally, by a sense of duty and self-sacrifice, they played a crucial part in the creation of the map of modern Britain. For that, if for nothing else, they are worthy of our attention.

NOTES

1. Currency. Before decimalisation in 1971 Scotland and England used the same monetary system of a pound (£) divided into 20 shillings (s), each of which comprised 12 pennies (d). One merk ('mark' in England), a unit of accounting rather than a coin, was worth two-thirds of a pound (13s 4d). Scottish and English silver pennies, the basic coins, were originally of equal value. However, devaluation of the Scottish currency occurred over the years on roughly the following basis:

In 1390 £1 English was worth £2 Scots

1450 £1 English was worth £3 Scots

1500 £1 English was worth £4 Scots

1560 £1 English was worth £5 Scots

1600 £1 English was worth £12 Scots The 1600 rate was maintained until 1707 when the two were in theory amalgamated into a single currency.

2. The Calendar. The Julian calendar was employed throughout Great Britain until 1751 when the Gregorian calendar was adopted. The change involved moving the date forward and a 'loss' of 11 days, so there can be some confusion over the exact timing of events which took place before the alteration. They may be given correctly in either the Julian (Old Style) or Gregorian (New Style) calendar.

3. Stewart/Stuart. The surname Stewart (from steward) presented problems for the French, Scotland's partners in the Auld Alliance, who were unaccustomed to the letter 'W'. Mary Queen of Scots and others with close French connections overcame the difficulty by altering the spelling of their name to Stuart. This variation was used by the royal family, although it is still customary to refer to them as Stewarts while they ruled only in Scotland but as Stuarts after the Union of the Crowns in 1603.

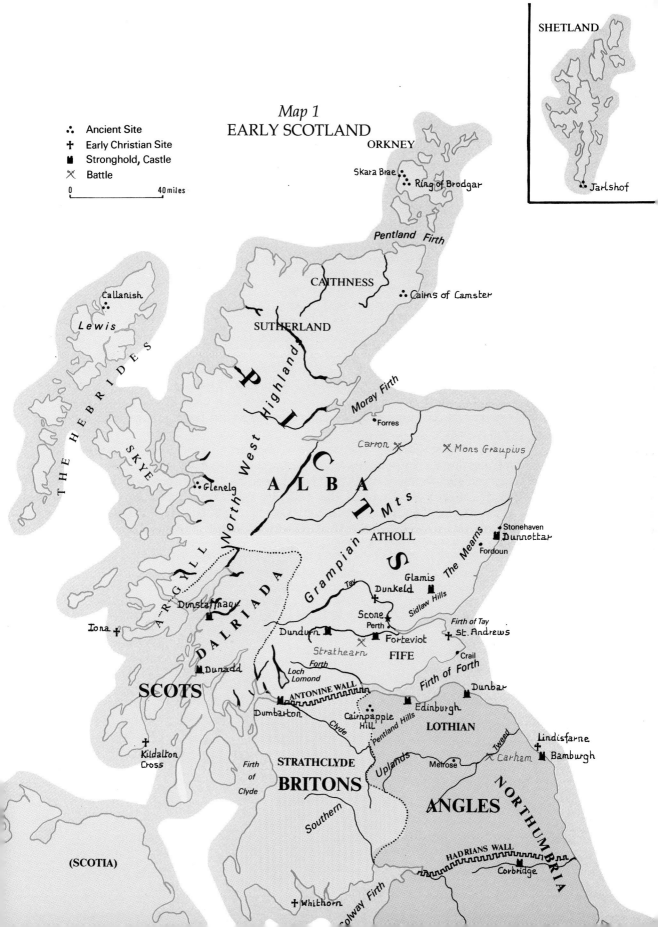

Map 1
EARLY SCOTLAND

∴ Ancient Site
✝ Early Christian Site
▲ Stronghold, Castle
✕ Battle

0 _____ 40 miles

SHETLAND

Jarlshof

ORKNEY

Skara Brae
Ring of Brodgar

Pentland Firth

CAITHNESS

∴ Cairns of Camster

Callanish

Lewis

SUTHERLAND

THE HEBRIDES

SKYE

P I C *Highland*

North West

Moray Firth

•Forres

Carron ✕

✕ Mons Graupius

∴ •Glenelg

A L B A

T

•Stonehaven
▲ Dunnottar
•Fordoun

ATHOLL

Grampian Mts

The Mearns

Iona ✝

ARGYLL

▲ Dunstaffnage

DALRIADA

Dundurn ▲

Scone ★
•Perth

Dunkeld ✝

Tay

Glamis

Sidlaw Hills

Firth of Tay
✝ St. Andrews

✕ Forteviot

Stratheam

FIFE

•Crail

SCOTS

▲ Dunadd

Forth

Loch
Lomond

ANTONINE WALL

Dumbarton

Cairnpapple
Hill

Edinburgh

Pentland Hills

LOTHIAN

Dunbar ▲

Firth of Forth

Lindisfarne ✝
▲ Bamburgh

✝ Kildalton
Cross

Clyde

STRATHCLYDE

Tweed

✕ Carham

NORTHUMBRIA

*Firth
of
Clyde*

BRITONS

Melrose•

Uplands

ANGLES

Southern

HADRIANS WALL

(SCOTIA)

✝ •Whithorn

Solway Firth

▲ Corbridge

The remarkably well preserved remains of a Stone Age dwelling at Skara Brae, Orkney, which date from about 1500BC. For hundreds of years the settlement was preserved from the despoilation of the elements and plunderers by a covering of sand. The purpose of the curious stone couches shown in this picture has never been satisfactorily explained. The village, which numbered only about 30 people, is the best surviving example of its kind in Britain.

THE EMERGENCE OF A KINGDOM
from earliest times to c. 841

Giant heavings and eruptions in the earth's crust established the familiar ragged outline of Scotland many millions of years ago. Four successive ice ages then smoothed the rugged landscape, leaving it by about 10,000BC much as we find it today, although the work of man and changes in climate have considerably altered the covering vegetation.

The principal geographical feature of Scotland is a fundamental division between the mountainous Highlands, rising north of a line running approximately north-east from Loch Lomond to Stonehaven, and the more pastoral Lowlands. There is no such obvious natural boundary further south, and the present frontier with England was determined only after centuries of warfare.

The Highland area is not universally inhospitable; many of the Western Isles and the area around the Moray Firth are warm and fertile. Furthermore, the Lowlands embrace the bleak hills of the Southern Uplands as well as rich farmland. To the visitor from the south, however, the overall physical impression of Scotland is one of hostility. Dark mountains are never out of sight. Even well into the eighteenth century it was not the sort of country that the English liked to visit. Scotland frightened them.

The effect of Scotland's mountainous terrain on its history has been twofold. Like Switzerland, it has proved difficult to unite under a single government. At the same time invaders have found it an almost impossible nation to subdue.

The country's original inhabitants arrived about 6000BC as settlers in a hitherto virgin and heavily forested land. They probably came by boat, first as scavengers and summer visitors, then as cave-dwelling hunters. The earliest known site of human habitation is at Morton in Fife. But as little is known of these men and women of the Middle Stone Age, we can only guess how they spent their precarious lives.

By 4000BC a new people had settled in Scotland. Their Mediterranean forbears had learned the techniques of agriculture and as they cleared land for farming the slow but inexorable process of deforestation began. Quite remarkable evidence of this civilisation has been uncovered at Skara Brae on Orkney. The inhabitants kept cattle and sheep, made pottery, and by 2000BC were living in a manner that was quite as civilised as that of their contemporaries in southern Europe, whom we all too readily assume to have been considerably more advanced.

Stone Age society was revolutionised in the second millenium BC by the Beaker people, bronze-working engineers from northern Europe. Their impressive stone circles, such as that at Callanish on the Isle of Lewis, remain to this day a source of mystery and admiration. In the sixth century BC the Celts, the last pre-Roman settlers, reached Scotland. They were fair-haired farmers and metal workers, organised in a matriarchal society which traded extensively with tribes in neighbouring lands. Despite the pejorative overtones of the word 'Barbarians', a term the Romans employed for all those living outside their empire, the way of life of the seventeen tribes of 'Picti' at the time of the birth of Christ was far from primitive. But they were too disunited for us to be able to recognise one of their leaders as monarch of all Scotland.

The Romans were conquerors and imperialists. Apart from the need to secure their frontier and give a certain neat symmetry to their empire, there was no logical incentive for them to occupy the poor and largely desolate northern part of the British Isles. But on several occasions they undertook the subjection of Scotland. In 80AD Emperor Agricola reached the Tay, building a chain of forts from the Clyde to the Forth. Three years later he pushed up to the Moray Firth, destroying a vast army of the local chieftain Calgacus at Mons Graupius in 84AD before being recalled to Rome. By 123AD incursions from Scotland had become serious enough for the Romans to construct the magnificent defensive line known as Hadrian's Wall. Twenty years later they were building another less formidable barrier, the Antonine Wall, much further north. In 200AD Severus made a final attempt to vanquish permanently the Pictish tribes of Scotland. Like Agricola, he occupied Morayshire for a while before retiring south. Although the tribes they met — mostly Picts as far as we can gather — were no match for them in open battle, the Romans never conquered Scotland. When their empire finally began to crumble and the legions were withdrawn from Britain they left tangible remains in the form of their walls and more than 1000 miles of fine roads. But their most signficant effect on Scotland was to unite the hitherto disparate tribes into what were essentially four distinct groups, or kingdoms.

The Picts controlled most of Scotland. Their sparsely populated territory stretched from the Pentland Firth in the north to the Pentland hills near Edinburgh. Theirs was not, however, a single united realm. In the eighth century the Venerable Bede spoke of two groups of Picts, north and south, and it was not until about this time that King Brude was recognised as the first chief of all the Pictish people. The Picts are an obscure and elusive people. No one really knows where they came from, or what happened to them. They spoke two languages. One is 'P. Celtic' (related to the Welsh, Cornish and Breton); the other resembles no other Indo-European tongue. By the eleventh century they had ceased to exist as an identifiable entity. We are left with no written language, but with a remarkable series of carved stones and a tradition of matrilineal descent still permissible in some Scottish families.

The Kingdom of the Angles, known as Northumbria, was situated south of Pictland, in Lothian. These warlike people of German descent had established Bamburgh as one of their major centres in the sixth century, then extended their control over neighbouring territory. In little over 100 years they

Even the Romans were unable to subdue Scotland. The Antonine wall ran from the Firth of Forth to the Clyde marking the furthest limit of permanent Roman occupation. It was strongly built in 143AD using earth on stone foundations and remains Scotland's most important and accessible piece of Roman construction.

had expanded to the west, to the south into Northumberland, and north as far as the river Forth. Yet in so doing they had probably overreached themselves, for they were easy prey for marauding Scandinavians in the next century.

Roman traditions survived longest in the British kingdom of Strathclyde. At one time it extended from the Clyde to north Wales, with Dumbarton as its capital. It was not a coherently organised state, but rather a collection of people of the same racial and cultural background, a strand of which was Christian. They had little influence on what was eventually to become the Kingdom of Scotland, but one family name, Wallace (from Walensis, meaning a Briton of Strathclyde), was to feature strongly in future Scottish history. One of their kings, Coel, remains forever enshrined in the literature of English nursery rhymes as Old King Cole.

Ironically the Scots, who were eventually to give their name to the whole of the country they settled in, came from Ireland. They were a warlike and aggressive people of Celtic origin. In about 500AD they invaded western Scotland north of the Clyde under the leadership of Fergus Mor, and established Dunadd in Argyll as the capital of their kingdom, which was known as Dalriada (Dal Riata) or Scotia. However, by the seventh century they still had as many as seven separate tribal family leaders. Initially they were subject to the superior power of the Picts to their east. In Dunadd there remains a vast rock, carved with a boar and a footprint, which was probably the place where Scottish kings were inaugurated. Shoes played an important part in this ceremony, a tradition which has been handed down in the tale of Cinderella.

The Scottish king Kenneth MacAlpin is generally accepted as the first true monarch of Scotland. But the picture of his inheritance is not complete without reference to two important influences: Christianity and the Vikings.

There is evidence from as early as 208AD that Christian beliefs in some form or another were held by the people living north of Hadrian's Wall. After the retreat of the Romans, however, these Christians had little contact with the mother church until the arrival in the fourth century of St Ninian, a Briton who had been to Rome. He founded a cell at Whithorn in Wigtownshire then travelled extensively, preaching and teaching. Despite his widespread influence and that engendered by the visit of St Patrick to Strathclyde in about 480, most of the inhabitants of Scotland remained loyal to their pagan gods and traditions. It was not until 563, when St Columba set foot on Scottish soil from Ireland, that a comprehensive conversion of the country began. Columba, who at the age of 42 had crossed the Irish sea in a coracle, was a tough and practical politician as well as a religious leader, and the faith he preached proved a major force in uniting the people of Scotland. Working from a base on the island of Iona, St Columba and his disciples were remarkably successful in spreading their gospel among the warring tribes. They founded several monasteries, for theirs was a monastic not a parochial church, and by about 800 all the Scottish kingdoms were nominally Christian. But this Celtic church was at odds with Rome over several issues, such as the date of Easter. So at a synod held in Whitby in 663, Saxon delegates successfully insisted that their precocious but poorly organised northern child accept orthodox ecclesiastical rules. It is said that while the Roman church gave law to Scottish Christianity, from the Celtic church it learned love.

In 793 the Vikings sacked the monastery at Lindisfarne, situated off the coast of Northumbria. Two years later Iona suffered the same fate. These raiders were not savage barbarians bent solely on rape and pillage, neither were they anti-Christian. To Orkney and Shetland they came as settlers, bringing their wives with them. But the gold and silver treasures of the monasteries were tempting targets for the marauders, and the chronicles of these times were written by monks. So the Vikings have had, as we would say, 'a bad press'.

By the middle of the ninth century the situation in southern Scotland was precarious, particularly in Dalriada. The Scots were being hard pressed from the sea by increasingly bold Viking incursions. At the same time the Picts were finding it difficult to withstand Danish assaults on the east coast. These were forcing the Picts into westward migration, away from the danger zones. Beset thus on either side, there was a real possibility that the kingdom of Dalriada might disappear altogether.

THE HOUSE OF ALPIN

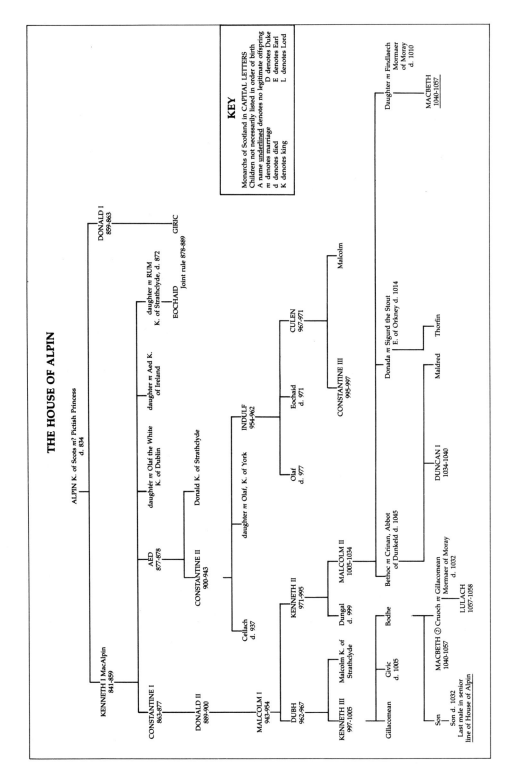

ALPIN K. of Scots m? Pictish Princess
d. 834

KENNETH I MacAlpin
841-859

DONALD I
859-863

CONSTANTINE I
863-877

AED
877-878

daughter m Olaf the White
K. of Dublin

daughter m Aed K.
of Ireland

daughter m RUM
K. of Strathclyde, d. 872

EOCHAID
Joint rule 878-889

GIRIC

DONALD II
889-900

CONSTANTINE II
900-943

Donald K. of Strathclyde

daughter m Olaf, K. of York

MALCOLM I
943-954

Cellach
d. 937

INDULF
954-962

Olaf
d. 977

Eochaid
d. 971

CULEN
967-971

CONSTANTINE III
995-997

Malcolm

DUBH
962-967

KENNETH II
971-995

Dungal
d. 999

MALCOLM II
1005-1034

Bethoc m Crinan, Abbot
of Dunkeld d. 1045

DUNCAN I
1034-1040

Donada m Sigurd the Stout
E. of Orkney d. 1014

Thorfin

Daughter m Findlaech
Mormaer of Moray
d. 1010

MACBETH
1040-1057

KENNETH III
997-1005

Malcolm K. of
Strathclyde

Bodhe

Givic
d. 1005

MACBETH ① Cruoch m Gillacomean
1040-1057   Mormaer of Moray
                 d. 1032

LULACH
1057-1058

Maldred

Gillacomean

Son

Son d. 1032
Last male in senior
line of House of Alpin

THE HOUSE OF ALPIN
c. 841 - 1034

Much of the history of the House of Alpin has been lost forever, and what remains is an obscure blend of fact and legend. Several of the dates given in the following pages, for example, are the subject of scholarly dispute. Yet it was under the vigorous but harsh rule of these men of Irish origin that the peoples of Scotland were forged into a single nation more than 1000 years ago.

KENNETH MACALPIN (KENNETH I)
c. 841 - c. 859

Born: ?. Died: c. 859. Marriage: ?. Children: Constantine, Aed and three daughters.

Almost nothing is known of Kenneth's mysterious father, Alpin, who founded the first dynasty of Scottish monarchs. He may not even have been a king of Dalriada. Certainly there is no truth whatsoever in the wonderfully contrived line of descent, constructed later from myth and downright lies to prove the superiority of the Scots over both the Picts and the English, which traced the House of Alpin back to the ancient Greeks, and eventually to Noah.

Alpin was killed in 834, fighting the Picts in Galloway. Kenneth, who had been born on Iona, immediately succeeded to the throne of Galloway, then to the hard-pressed Dalriada in about 841. We should not visualise Kenneth sitting on a throne in a fairy-tale palace imperiously issuing commands to his courtiers, for he was really little more than the most powerful of a number of warrior chiefs. His authority rested more upon his wit and skill as a fighter than upon respect for his title. Nevertheless, his position entitled him to certain taxes, fines and forfeitures as well as to military service, and the king's power was enhanced by a general recognition that he was lord of all the country. His personal wealth emanated from the royal estates, or demense. In times of trouble it was around the figure of the king that men gathered.

It is highly unlikely that Kenneth was crowned king. There was no formal papal blessing upon the coronation of a Scottish king until Pope John XXII recognised David II in 1329. A more likely en-kinging ceremony involved the new monarch being set upon a significant stone. Kings may later have worn a crown for certain formal occasions but otherwise peripatetic monarchs, who spent much of their hectic lives in the saddle, saw little purpose in displaying the symbolic but impractical circlet.

Kenneth's master stroke, upon which his reputation largely rests, was being accepted as king of the Picts in about 843, thus uniting two of the four major Scottish power blocs. The new title probably came to him via his mother, a Pictish princess, for descent among these people was matrilineal. He was proclaimed king on Moot Hill at Scone, a Pictish sacred place. He later enhanced the settlement's importance by bringing to it the celebrated 'Lia Fail' or Stone of Destiny. Upon this stone, which according to legend had originally been the pillow of Jacob or St Columba, the kings of Scotland were inaugurated until Edward III removed it to Westminster Abbey in 1296. Superstition held that where this stone was, there the rightful king of Scots would be also, and that the Scots would be free as long as they were ruled by a monarch proclaimed on the stone, as Elizabeth II was in 1953.

The united kingdom of the Picts and Scots was known sometimes simply as Scotia, but more usually as Alba. The title of Duke of Albany, which features in Shakespeare's King Lear, originates from this name.

The fate of the Picts is a mystery. Quite simply, they vanish from history. One chronicler stated that Kenneth helped this process by inviting many of their nobility to a magnificent drunken feast at his Forteviot palace, then slaughtered them as they staggered defenceless. Although very much in keeping with the sort of unscrupulous behaviour to be expected of a successful king in those ruthless times, the story is probably apocryphal. What is more likely is that, as one writer puts it, the 'Pictish system of government was peacefully bred out of existence'. In other words, caught between the Scots and the Norsemen, and perhaps with their culture already ailing, the Picts were simply absorbed by their more vigorous neighbours. The Gaelic of the Scots became the dominant language.

Although some English historians have dubbed Kenneth I the 'Scottish Alfred' for his combination of military, scholarly and organisational skills, there is little specific evidence for such a claim. Indeed, Scots may wonder why the parallel is made this way round: would it not be more accurate to call Alfred, who did not succeed to the throne of Wessex until 871, the 'English MacAlpin'? Kenneth's 'marvellous astuteness' is referred to by one chronicler, and the king certainly demonstrated political skill in the influential marriages he arranged for his daughters. He also had a somewhat vague reputation as a law-giver. As far as we can tell, Kenneth was relatively successful at resisting Danish attacks, wisely moving the administrative centres of his kingdom from the vulnerable fortesses of Dunadd and Dunstaffnage in the west to Scone and Forteviot, near present-day Perth. Dunkeld became the new spiritual capital — graced with the holy relics of St Columba, which were transferred from beleaguered Iona.

Danish incursions had isolated the countryside south of the Forth from English assistance and Kenneth took advantage of the situation to invade the territory six times. Although he is reported to have burned Dunbar and Melrose he never held Lothian for long, perhaps because he was continually having to abandon his southward thrusts to beat off Norse assaults to his rear. No doubt exhausted by years of struggle to control his inheritance, he eventually died of cancer in 859, leaving the kingdom to his brother Donald.

DONALD I
c. 859 - 863

Born: ?. Died: 863. Marriage: ?. Child: Giric.

The succession of Donald I after his brother Kenneth can be understood only in the context of the Celtic practice of tanistry. This held that, upon the death of a king, the throne could pass to anyone who was 'derbfine' — of reasonably close kindred to the previous monarch. This formula for regular family bloodbaths was, however, defined a little more tightly by the insistance that the heir be male, and 'rigdomnae', in other words of suitable calibre to be king. In an effort to lessen the jealousies and conflicts which this somewhat Darwinian law of succession inevitably tended to produce, the custom had arisen for kings to nominate their intended successor — the 'tanaise' — during their reign. Although this did not always solve the problem, and could on occasion exacerbate it, it did help to prevent civil war from being the automatic concomitant of a monarch's death. Nevertheless, 10 of the 14 kings who ruled Alba between 943 and 1097 were murdered. Only then was primogeniture generally accepted.

If we are to believe the chronicles, Donald's short reign was free from Viking raids but his death at Scone in 863 may have been the result of foul play. Kenneth MacAlpin's attempts to impose a degree of law and order on the unruly kingdom were furthered when Donald confirmed the ancient 'rights and laws' of a Dalriadic predecessor, Aed, at Forteviot.

Within the grounds of Scone Palace (built 1803-1808 for the Earls of Mansfield) can be found Moot Hill. To this site Kenneth MacAlpin, the monarch who first united the Picts with the Scots into the kingdom of Alba (later Scotia), brought the Stone of Destiny, which was kept in the abbey nearby. Many generations of Scottish monarchs were inaugurated — a ceremony which later came to involve crowning — upon Moot Hill.

CONSTANTINE I
863 - c. 877

Born: ?. Died: c. 877. Marriage: ?. Child: Donald.

Constantine I seems to have been very much a typical ninth- century warrior king. Most of his energies were spent combating Viking assaults or attempting to extend his authority south of the Forth-Clyde line. In 872 Constantine arranged for the murder of Run, King of Strathclyde, who was married to one of Constantine's sisters, and it is possible that at this time the more southerly kingdom became dependent upon Scotia.

Constantine faced his first Norse attack in 864, when he had been king for scarcely a year. It was made by Olaf the White from Dublin, another of Constantine's brothers-in-law. Olaf may have been killed by Constantine himself, but his exact fate is uncertain. Whatever happened, by 871 he had ceased to be a threat. In 875 another colour-coded Dane, Thorsten the Red, was also defeated and killed by Constantine. At other times the king was less confident, buying peace with the assailants by paying tribute, a tactic supposedly to have been used by the English King Ethelred (the 'Unready') in the eleventh century.

In the end, however, the Danes had their revenge. A sinister party known as the Black Strangers had been driven from Dublin and had established themselves in Fife. From here they launched raids on Constantine, eventually slaying him in battle. Tradition has it that he met his end in the long Black Cave (or Cove?) near Crail in Fife.

AED
c. 877 - 878

Born: ?. Died: 878. Marriage: ?. Children: Constantine and Donald.

We are not certain whom Constantine I designated as his tanaise. His younger brother, Aed (or Whitefoot) held the throne for only a year before he was killed in 878 at Strathallan by his cousin Giric (sometimes known by his anglicised title of Gregory the Great). This untimely death, during a period when the kingdom must have needed to marshal all available resources to counter Viking incursions, serves only to highlight the unsatisfactory nature of the law of tanistry and the precariousness of royal authority.

However, it would be wrong to infer from the seemingly incessant bloodletting among its chiefs that we are dealing with a crude and uncultured society. Gaelic has given us Europe's oldest post-Roman vernacular literature. Harp music and beautifully illuminated manuscripts suggest that a rich and sensitive culture endured behind the clashes and cries of the battlefields.

EOCHAID AND GIRIC
878 - c. 889

We know virtually no personal details of these two kings. As far as we can tell, King Aed was succeeded by his nephew Eochaid and his cousin Giric (or Gregory), who ruled as joint monarchs. The accession of Eochaid, the son of one of Kenneth MacAlpin's daughters by her marriage to Run, King of Strathclyde, suggests that the Pictish matrilineal law of succession had not entirely died out. Giric was the son of MacAlpin's brother, Donald I.

The exact nature of this concurrent rule is not known. Perhaps Giric acted as regent for the under-age Eochaid, and shared his title of king? On the other hand, the two men may have been rivals. Eochaid remains a shadowy figure, little more than a somewhat obscure name; but Giric, who was of British descent, seems to fit more closely into the prevailing pattern of ruthless soldier kings. It was he who killed Aed to make the throne available in 878. Later he is supposed to have launched a successful invasion of Northumbria, which led to his controlling large areas south of the Forth for a while.

Other sources indicate that Giric was something of an ecclesiastical patron, who released the church from the burden of paying the duties and dues charged to secular landlords. In the end, though, whatever favour he may have found among the religious was of little temporal help, for in 889 both kings were deposed, and Giric was killed at Dundurn in Perthshire.

DONALD II
889 - 900

Born: ?. Died: 900. Marriage: ?. Child: Malcolm.

After the joint rule of Eochaid and Giric the Scottish throne alternated between two branches, or segments, of the ruling house. Each stemmed from a son of Kenneth MacAlpin, one from Constantine I, the other from Aed.

Constantine's son Donald II had the misfortune to reign during the period when Danish asaults were at their most unrelieved. To the south the successors to the celebrated Danish leader Guthrum seized Northumbria, threatening the Scots and cutting them off from contact with England. At roughly the same time the whole of northern Scotland fell to Sigura (Sigurd 'the Mighty'). Even the almost impregnable fortress of Dunnottar fell into Danish hands. Sigura emphasised his victory by cutting off the head of his defeated adversary, Melbrigda Tonn, and hanging it from his saddle. The gesture proved unfortunate. As the gory trophy banged around against the flank of his horse, one of the teeth pierced Sigura's leg and led to his painful death from blood poisoning. Subsequent sagas gave Melbrigda Tonn the simple but appropriate nickname of 'The Tooth'.

Exhausted by years of fighting, Donald himself died in 900, either at Dunnottar or near Forres. Poison was suspected.

CONSTANTINE II
900 - 943

Born: ?. Died: 952. Marriage: ?. Children: Indulf, Cellach and a daughter.

Constantine II was the eldest son of Aed. His long reign is one of the most significant in the early history of Scotland. During the first part of his 43-year occupation of the throne of Alba the Scots both resisted Danish incursions and secured their influence south of the Firth-Clyde line. This brought them face to face with the emergent Anglo-Saxon kingdom of England for the first time and instigated a pattern of invasion and resistance which was to prove so central a feature of Scottish history for the ensuing centuries.

It is probable that Strathclyde had been subject to Scottish suzerainty since about 872, so when the last British king of Strathclyde died in 908 and the throne passed to Constantine's brother Donald, the House of Alpin's control was confirmed. Constantine's influence did not remain unchallenged for long.

The Norse had plundered Dunkeld in the third year of Constantine's reign, but they withdrew in 904 after a defeat at Strathearn. In 912 we find Constantine again confronting the Scandinavian threat, this time south of Lothian, an area over which he and his predecessors may well have exercised some sort of control for more than 40 years. In alliance with the Northumbrians, Constantine advanced as far as Corbridge in 915, then retreated north. A similar sequence of events took place about three years later and by 920 Rognvald, a

The spendidly sited Dunnottar Castle just to the south of Stonehaven has featured prominently in Scottish history from the earliest times. Owing to the fact that it is almost entirely shielded by the sea breaking at the base of precipitous cliffs, capture of the castle has always been hazardous. Wallace achieved it, so did Cromwellian troops, but the success of the Danes in the reign of Donald II (889-900) was even more remarkable.

Danish invader from Ireland, had firmly established himself in York. The ding-dong fighting was finally brought to a close in 927 when the talented English king Athelstan united all the Danes' foes to drive them out. This victory brought Constantine even greater danger: with the Scandinavian buffer-state removed, he now had a common frontier with England.

However, for a time relations between the two kingdoms seemed quite peaceful and in 927 Athelstan even agreed to become godfather to Constantine's son. But within five years the fragile harmony was shattered. Athelstan invaded Scotland as far north as Dunnottar and demanded Constantine's son as a hostage before he would withdraw. Undaunted, three years later the ambitious King of Scots struck south, this time at the head of a motley coalition of Danes from Dublin and Northumbria, and Britons from Strathclyde. But they were no match for Athelstan's experienced and ordered army. In 937 the Scots and their allies were slaughtered at Brunanburgh (the site of the battle has never been satisfactorily identified), a fight which was triumphantly recorded in the Anglo-Saxon Chronicle.

Constantine never recovered from the humiliation suffered at Brunanburgh. Athelstan installed Eric Bloodaxe as Earl of Northumbria and Alba's influence over Strathclyde and Lothian waned. In 941 Danish assaults again threatened, this time as far north as Dunbar.

Constantine had always shown a keen interest in church affairs. In 906 he engineered the union of the Pictish and Scottish churches under Cellach, the Bishop of St Andrews, to whose seat he had transferred the precious relics of St Columba from Dunkeld. No doubt weary of fighting and having seen his earlier successes swept aside, in 943 Constantine retired to the monastery of St Andrews. Although this abdication may not have been entirely voluntary, he remained in this holy retreat for the remaining nine years of his life.

MALCOLM 1
943 - 954

Born: ?. Died: 954. Marriage: ?. Children: Dubh and Kenneth.

Malcolm I was the second cousin and tanaise of his predecessor, Constantine II. The fact that his accession was accepted by Constantine's more immediate family suggests that Malcolm possessed the necessary kingly qualities of leadership and military prowess. As soon as they came to the throne Scottish kings of the early medieval period were under considerable pressure to launch aggressive raids on their neighbours in order to exert their authority and to provide their supporters with an opportunity for booty.

Malcolm was no exception. In the year of his accession he led a successful expedition north, capturing Moray and slaughtering the local king. This brought Moray firmly under the rule of the House of Alpin for the first time.

In the early years of his reign Malcolm allied with the English to combat the serious threat of Scandinavian attack from Ireland. In return for recognition as ruler of Cumbria, Malcolm agreed to help his southern neighbour 'on both sea and land'. But in 950, probably egged on by the venerable ex-King Constantine, who was still exercising some authority from his cloistered retreat at St Andrews, Malcolm moved into England, harrying Northumbria as far south as the Tees. However, the people of Moray used the king's absence to launch a massive revolt and when Malcolm returned north to deal with them they managed to kill him at Fordoun in the Mearns. The English King Eadred then recaptured Northumbria. Although from the perspective of the late twentieth century the ceaseless, almost ritual warfare of the early Scottish kings appears rather futile, it is worth remembering that the scale of fighting was usually very small — an 'army' might have comprised little more than a few hundred warriors — and a king who did not seek to further his kingdom's interests by force of arms was clearly failing in his duty.

INDULF
954 - 962

Born: ?. Died: 962. Marriage: ?. Children: Culen, Olaf and Eochaid.

After Malcolm's death the throne of Alba passed to Constantine II's son, Indulf. He may well have been the child at whose christening in 927 the King of England had stood as godfather.

From the little that we know of it, Indulf's reign was, with a single exception, marked by the familiar pattern of raid and counter-raid carried out between Danes, Scots and English across northern Northumbria. The one development of enduring significance was Indulf's capture of the mighty fortress of Edinburgh (Dun Eden) from Edwin the Anglian.

The exact nature of Indulf's demise is uncertain. He may have emulated his father by retiring to the monastery at St Andrews, or he may have been killed there by a Danish force which had been driven out of York by the English. All we know for certain is that after 962 Indulf was no longer king of Alba.

DUBH (or DUFF)
962 - c. 967

Born: ?. Died: c. 967. Marriage: ?. Children: Kenneth and Malcolm.

The tricky question of the succession re-emerged once again during the brief reign of Dubh 'the black'. Indulf's son Culen, known somewhat unflatteringly as 'the whelp', twice fought Dubh for the throne. Dubh overcame the first challenge, which was made in Atholl, and slew its leaders, the Abbot of Dunkeld and the Mormaer of Atholl. (Mormaer was a title akin to the English earl or thane.)

But in 967 Dubh was less fortunate. He was killed at Forres in Moray, leaving his tanaise Culen to take over the kingship. Legend has it that for a while Dubh's body lay undiscovered under a bridge, and the sun did not shine until the corpse was located and buried. An eclipse on 10th July 967 may not be unconnected with this somewhat bizarre story.

CULEN
c. 967 - 971

Born: ?. Died: 971. Marriage: ?. Children: Constantine and Malcolm.

Culen 'the whelp' is an obscure figure whose reign was both short and bloody. After seizing the throne from Dubh, he attempted to regain control over Strathclyde. During the campaign he killed the brother of Strathclyde's British king, Rhiderch, and seized his daughter. The British soon had their revenge when Rhiderch slew 'the whelp' in Lothian. This cleared the way for Dubh's brother, Kenneth, to try his luck on the precarious throne of Alba.

'Edinburgh Castle and the Nor Loch' by Alexander Nasmyth. Although the great fortification we see today is of much later construction, the capture of Edinburgh in the reign of King Indulf (954-962) marked an important step in the southward expansion of the kingdom of Alba. The loch was filled in 1816.

KENNETH II
971 - 995

Born: ?. Died: 995. Marriage: ?. Children: Dungal and Malcolm.

In an age of almost perpetual warfare and civil strife the reign of Kenneth seems remarkable for its uneventfulness. This may testify to Kenneth's diplomatic skills, to his lack of ambition, or even to our lack of information. Following the humiliating death of Culen at the hands of the people of Strathclyde, the new king tried unsuccessfully to avenge this slur on the House of Alpin. When his invasion failed, Kenneth listened to more pacific counsels and it was another 20 years before he again attempted to expand his kingdom through military force.

Kenneth maintained friendly relations with England. He was the most distinguished member of a crew of eight kings who in 873 rowed King Edgar up the river Dee at Chester. Although the pageant was supposed to be in honour of John the Baptist, its significance concerning Kenneth's relationship with Edgar was plain for all to see. In return for accepting the English king as his lord, Kenneth was recognised as King of Lothian and loaded with other honours, such as English manors whose riches could sustain him on future visits to Edgar's court. Four years later Kenneth strengthened his position at home by murdering Culen's brother Olaf, a possible rival claimant to the throne.

Only in 994 was Kenneth tempted to strike south into Northumbria. The venture was a failure, however, and he soon had to return home to face the inevitable uprising which had broken out in his absence.

There is a story that Kenneth met a startling death. For a long time the Scottish kings had found the Mearns a difficult area to control and in attempting to enforce his authority there Kenneth had slain the son of Finella, the wife of the mormaer of the Mearns. The embittered woman planned a sinister revenge. In her castle she had a copper tower built, bedecked inside with rich and elaborate tapestries. Several loaded crossbows were secured behind these hangings. She then placed a statue of a king holding a golden apple in the centre of the room, at the point where the bows were aimed. Her engineers devised a mechanical trip by which removal of the apple triggered off the crossbows.

With the trap thus set, Kenneth was invited to stay. Finella proved a charming hostess. She entertained the king to a grand banquet at which minstrels played and expensive wines flowed freely. Later that night she took her tipsy guest by the hand and drew him to the copper tower where she invited him to take the golden apple as a token of their lasting reconciliation.

The unsuspecting Kenneth lurched forward, grabbed the apple, and perished like some Scottish St Sebastian in a deadly hail of arrows.

CONSTANTINE III
995 - 997

Born: ?. Died: 997. Marriage: ?. Children: ?.

The reign of Culen's son, Constantine III, was as unsuccessful as it was brief. History leaves no record of his personality or achievements and even the manner of his death at Rathinveramon is obscure. Some say that he was killed by an illegitimate son of Malcolm I, others believe that Dubh's son Kenneth undertook the deed. Whoever was responsible, Constantine's death marks a low point in the early story of the Scottish monarchy. The succession was left in chaos at a time when the emergent nation urgently needed a stable figure about whom it could rally to resist English and Norse incursions.

KENNETH III
997 - 1005

Born: ?. Died: 1005. Marriage: ?. Children: Gillacomean, Giric and Bodhe.

By the time of Kenneth III it was apparent that the law of tanistry was an unsuitable method of settling the succession for a kingdom which could not afford the luxury of constant civil disturbance. Kenneth, who was known as 'The Brown' (Donn) or 'The Grim', came from 'Strong Duncaith', an obscure fortress in the Sidlaw hills. Having terminated his predecessor's reign after only two years, he enjoyed the fruits of his ambition for only eight years before he too fell at the hands of a usurper. When Kenneth engaged in what had now become the almost obligatory pastime of Scottish kings, raiding northern England, he was easily repulsed. As a result of King Ethelred's retaliatory invasion Lothian was wrested from Scottish control. Thus, with most of the territory south of the Firth-Clyde line now lost and royal authority in the Highlands only spasmodically obeyed, it was probably just as well for Alba that, before any further disaster befell the kingdom, Kenneth was killed at Monzievaird, near the River Earn. His son Giric died with him.

A remarkably carved arch-stone found in the Water of May near Forteviot. The village near Perth was the site of the principal fort of Kenneth MacAlpin (c.841-c.859) and many of the kings of the House of Alpin enjoyed the royal residence here, set in a rich verdant valley.

The island of Iona off Mull in the Inner Hebrides is the site where in 563 St Columba landed from Ireland to begin the effective christianisation of Scotland. He established a monastery there and the holy island was chosen as a final resting place for no fewer than 48 Scottish monarchs, including the celebrated pair of Shakespearian adversaries, Duncan and Macbeth.

MALCOLM II
1005 - 1034

Born: c. 954. Died: 1034. Marriage: ?. Children: Bethoc, Donada and another daughter.

The dynasty founded by Kenneth MacAlpin came to a close with the long reign of Malcolm II. Although some members of the family had been scarcely more than bloodthirsty bandits, with little concept of government or law and order, by 1034 a reasonably clearly defined Scottish kingdom had emerged. The extent and cohesion of this realm owed much to the work of Malcolm II.

There was, however, little in the first few years of Malcolm's reign to suggest that his rule would be different from that of his imediate predecessors. Having won the throne by murdering Kenneth III and his son near Perth, Malcolm marched south on the obligatory rampage into England. While laying seige to Durham in an effort to get his hands on the treasures of St Cuthbert, he was defeated by Uhtred, Earl of Northumbria and driven north. Lothian remained in English hands.

Undaunted, Malcolm now turned his attention to his northern frontier, where the mormaer of Moray and Scandinavian invaders held sway. In 1008 Malcolm suffered a setback near Forres but two years later he won his first victory, 'ramscuttering' a Viking army at Carron, near Dufftown. No doubt aware of his somewhat uncertain military prowess, Malcolm proceeded to employ other methods to preserve his influence in this unruly part of his kingdom. His second daughter was probably married to Findlaech, the mormaer of Moray, while her younger sister Donada took Sigura 'the Stout', Earl of Orkney as a husband. The son of this marriage, Thorfin 'the Mighty', was later to control a huge northern earldom, which included Caithness, Sutherland, Orkney, Shetland and most of the Hebrides.

The union with Findlaech had a less happy outcome. In 1020 the unfortunate mormaer was slain by his nephews, one of whom, Gillacomean, was related by marriage to the royal family on Kenneth III's side. Gruoch, Gillacomean's wife, was Kenneth's granddaughter.

But no northern mormaer was safe for long and in 1032 Gillacomean and his men were burned to death. This freed his widow to marry Findlaech's son, Macbeth. The stage was thus set for what is surely the most famous of Scotland's royal blood feuds.

Meanwhile, Malcolm II had sought once more to consolidate his southern frontier, this time meeting with spectacular success. Assisted by Owen the Bald, the last independent King of Strathclyde, in 1018 Malcolm crushed Uhtred at Carham on Tweed. When Uhtred reported the disaster to King Cnut, the vanquished earl was promptly assassinated and Northumberland was given to his brother, Eadulf, who in turn ceded Lothian to Malcolm. Although much disputed in detail, the modern boundary between England and Scotland was thereby established. Malcolm was granted Lothian on condition that its language and customs were not interfered with, a stipulation which made the new acquisition the principle door through which future Anglo-Norman influence would enter Scotland.

Malcolm had no sons. To avoid a contested succession, therefore, he wished to pass on the throne to Duncan, the son of his eldest daughter, Bethoc. To this end he slaughtered the remaining male descendants of Kenneth III. When Malcolm finally died in 1035, aged over 80, Duncan was proclaimed king. Already in possession of Strathclyde, his considerable inheritance now stretched from the Tweed to the Moray Firth. The Scottish kingdom thus created remains an enduring monument to the unflagging efforts of the House of Alpin.

THE HOUSE OF DUNKELD 1034-1290

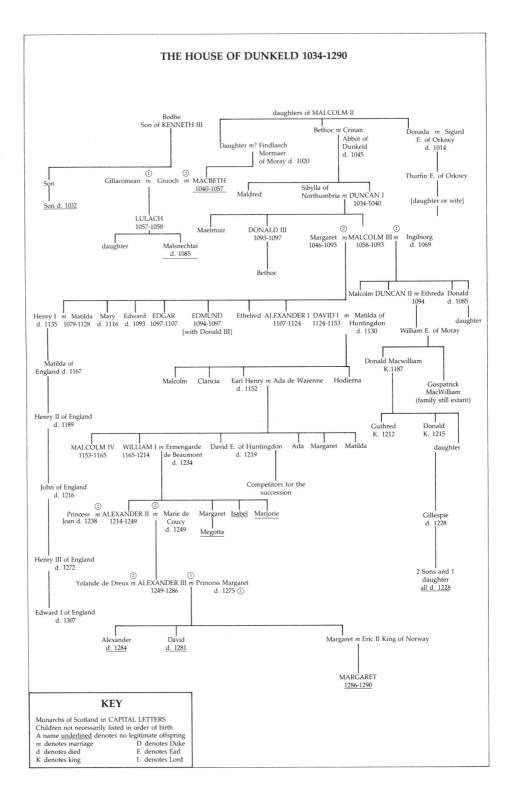

Bodhe
Son of KENNETH III

daughters of MALCOLM II

Bethoc *m* Crinan
Abbot of
Dunkeld
d. 1045

Daughter *m*? Findlaech
Mormaer
of Moray d. 1020

Donada *m* Sigurd
E. of Orkney
d. 1014

Thurfin E. of Orkney

Son

Son d. 1032

Gillacomean *m* Gruoch *m* MACBETH
(1)   (2)   1040-1057

Maldred

Sibylla of
Northumbria *m* DUNCAN I
1034-1040

[daughter or wife]

LULACH
1057-1058

Maelmuir

DONALD III
1093-1097

Margaret *m* MALCOLM III *m* Ingibiorg
1046-1093   (2) 1058-1093 (1) d. 1069

daughter

Malsnechtai
d. 1085

Bethoc

Malcolm DUNCAN II *m* Ethreda Donald
1094   d. 1085

Henry I *m* Matilda Mary   Edward EDGAR   EDMUND   Ethelred ALEXANDER I DAVID I *m* Matilda of   daughter
d. 1135 1079-1128 d. 1116 d. 1093 1097-1107   1094-1097   1107-1124 1124-1153   Huntingdon
                                                 [with Donald III]   d. 1130

                                                                                                    William E. of Moray

Matilda of
England d. 1167

Malcolm   Claricia   Earl Henry *m* Ada de Warenne   Hodierna

Donald Macwilliam
K.1187

Gospatrick
MacWilliam
(family still extant)

Henry II of England
d. 1189

MALCOLM IV   WILLIAM I *m* Ermengarde   David E. of Huntingdon   Ada   Margaret   Matilda
1153-1165   1165-1214   de Beaumont   d. 1219
                        d. 1234

Guthred
K. 1212

Donald
K. 1215

daughter

John of England
d. 1216

Competitors for the
succession

Princess *m* ALEXANDER II *m* Marie de   Margaret   Isabel   Marjorie
Joan d. 1238 (1) 1214-1249 (2) Coucy
                                  d. 1249

Megotta

Gillespie
d. 1228

Henry III of England
d. 1272

Yolande de Dreux *m* ALEXANDER III *m* Princess Margaret
(2)   1249-1286 (1) d. 1275 (1)

2 Sons and 1
daughter
all d. 1228

Edward I of England
d. 1307

Alexander
d. 1284

David
d. 1281

Margaret *m* Eric II King of Norway

MARGARET
1286-1290

THE HOUSE OF DUNKELD
1034 - 1290

Under a series of strong and competent monarchs from the House of Dunkeld, Scotland not only maintained her status as an independent state but grew to be one of the better governed nations of western Europe.

DUNCAN I
1034 - 1040

Born: 1001. Died: 1040. Marriage: Sibylla, a sister or cousin of Siward, Earl of Northumbria. Children: Maelmuir, Donald, Malcolm.

During the early medieval period the king was not only a figure of prestige and authority; he was also a target for every ambitious member of his family. As time went by, in both England and Scotland the institution of monarchy was endowed with religious significance in an effort to promote political stability. Opposition to the king or queen thus became a crime against both God and man. Such thinking was prevalent when William Shakespeare wrote Macbeth. Moreover, the playwright carefully distorted the few pieces of concrete information available to him in the interests of artistic and dramatic effect. King Duncan ('the Gracious') became a wise and gentle old man; his slayer Macbeth emerged as an ambitious soldier who had resorted not even to open combat but to 'murder most foul' to seize the crown. The recreation produced brilliant theatre, which also reflected the Elizabethan paranoia about rebellion, but it hardly accorded with the known facts.

Duncan was the tanaise and grandson of Malcolm II. His mother Bethoc had married Crinan, lay Abbot of Dunkeld. As Scottish monasticism was at a low ebb, the appointment of a magnate to a powerful abbacy was a sensible move. At least it ensured a man of some stature and ability in the key ecclesiastical post, while the elevation enabled Crinan to enjoy the fruits of high church office without the uncomfortable deprivations of the customary vows of chastity and poverty.

Bethoc and Crinan had two sons, Maldred and Duncan. For reasons which are not clear to us King Malcolm favoured the latter. On the death of Owen the Bold in 1018 Duncan had become King of Strathclyde, so when he was proclaimed King of Scotland in 1034 the kingdom of the south-west ceased to exist as an independent entity. Duncan's inheritance was thus larger than that

ORKNEY
(under Norse rule)

SHETLAND
(as Orkney)

Map 2
MEDIEVAL SCOTLAND

Pentland Firth

• Thurso

Lewis

CAITHNESS

Dornoch

ROSS

Moray Firth

Dunskeath

┼ Kinloss
Forres • Elgin

Redcastle

Inverness

Strathbogie
Essie •

Spey

MORAY

Kildrummy ╳ Aberdeen
Lumphanan
Dee

┼ Dunvegan
Skye

THE
HEBRIDES
(ceded to Norway)
1098-1267)

ARGYLL

Atholl Stracathro ╳ *The Mearns*

Brechin ┼ Montrose •

Dunstaffnage

Coupar
Angus ┼ • Forfar

• Oban

Iona ┼

Dunkeld

Scone

Dundee ┼ Arbroath

Firth of Tay

Dupplin Moor ╳ Perth

• Abernethy St. Andrews

Dunblane ┼

Stirling Br.

Stirling Dunfermline *Firth of Forth*

Bannockburn ╳ • Kinghorn

Loch
Lomond Inchcolm ┼

Dumbarton *Falkirk* ╳ Queensferry ┼ Dunbar ╳

Edinburgh • Musselburgh Coldingham ┼

Glasgow Holyrood ┼ Newbattle ┼ Halidon ╳ Berwick
Largs ╳ Hill

Tarbert Lanark *Tweed* Norham

Rothesay *Clyde* Melrose Birgham
Kelso Coldstream

Loudoun Hill ╳ Selkirk Roxburgh
Dryburgh ┼ Alnwick

Kintyre *Firth
of
Clyde* Ayr Jedburgh ┼

Hermitage THE BORDER

Lochmaben

Dumfries GALLOWAY Caerlaverock Newcastle

Sweetheart ┼

Wigtown Kirkcudbright Carlisle Durh

Whithorn ┼ *Solway Firth* *Neville's Cross* ╳

ENGLAND

MORAY Diocese
┼ Cathedral   ┼ Abbey
■ Castle   ╳ Battle
▪ Royal Burgh

0 _____ 25 miles

IRELAND

of any of his predecessors.

The young king of 33 was not the wise and respected governor described by the Bard. Duncan held his throne for only six years. Following unsuccessful sallies into northern England in 1039, he was killed in battle the next year by his more able cousin, Macbeth. The fight may well have taken place near Birnam Woods, Shakespeare's mobile venue for Macbeth's demise, for Duncan is said to have held court on Birnam Hill, near Dunkeld.

MACBETH
1040 - 1057

Born: c. 1005. Died: 1057. Marriage: Gruoch. No children.

There is no historical evidence to suggest that Macbeth (or Maelbeatha) was anything other than a most competent monarch. He was certainly not the hell-hound of theatrical production and it has been suggested that it was not even he who killed King Duncan but Duncan's cousin Thorfin, Earl of Orkney.

Macbeth's claim to the throne of Scotland was sound. His wife Gruoch was directly descended from Kenneth III, while his mother was probably Donalda, the middle of Malcolm II's three daughters. Moreover, when Macbeth came to the throne he was, like his predecessor Duncan, already an experienced governor, having been mormaer of the tough province of Moray since 1029. Tradition has it that it was in this part of the country that he met with the three witches, near Alves. He may well have had some sort of castle at Inverness.

Macbeth's inheritance was not an easy one. In the north he was threatened by the might of Thorfin; at home he had to deal with the thwarted ambitions of Crinan; and Duncan's young son Malcolm, who was sheltering with his powerful maternal relatives, the Siwards of Northumbria, was eager to win back the prize his father had lost. Crinan was the first to fall, killed by Macbeth in a fight near Dunkeld in 1045. The next year Macbeth appears temporarily to have lost control of Lothian to Earl Siward. The reverse was shortlived, however, for in 1050 Macbeth is recorded as being on pilgrimage in Rome, at the same time as Thorfin, his northern protagonist. It is possible that they were both seeking papal absolution for crimes previously committed. The clear inference from Macbeth's visit is that he was secure enough in his kingdom to leave it for several months. Evidence of his wealth, and perhaps of a liberal nature, is provided by a chronicler who tells us that Macbeth 'scattered money like seed among the poor' of the Eternal City.

Earl Siward 'the strong' was a renowned Viking warrior who, according to legend, was the product of the uncomfortable but effective coupling of a

Glamis Castle, Tayside. Although much of the present building is of seventeenth and eighteenth century construction, there may well have been some kind of stronghold here at the time of Macbeth. The castle acquired happier associations this century as one of the childhood residences of Queen Elizabeth, the Queen Mother.

woman with a white bear. After Macbeth's return from Italy, in 1054 Siward again used his military strength to press the claim of the exiled Malcolm to the Scottish throne. This time Macbeth was defeated at Scone and forced to cede to Malcolm large areas in the south of his kingdom. Although Siward died in 1055 — complaining bitterly that he was not perishing in battle as he would have liked, but ignominiously and in peace 'like a cow' — Malcolm was now strong enough to fight his own battles. He struck north in 1057, defeating Macbeth at Lumphanan in Aberdeenshire. The much-maligned king was not slain on the rugged summit of Dunsinane Hill, but probably in the far less glamorous Pell Bog.

LULACH
1057 - 1058

Born: 1032. Died: 1058. Marriage: ?. Children: Maelsnectai and a daughter.

King Lulach 'the simple' was only a distant blood relation of his predecessor, Macbeth. He was the son of Gruoch (Macbeth's wife) by her first husband Gillacomean. Macbeth's father was Findlaech, sometime mormaer of Moray. Gillacomean, his nephew, killed him in 1020 and took the title of mormaer for himself. Twelve years later Gillacomean and his followers were viciously burned to death. This freed Gruoch to marry Macbeth, the new mormaer. Shakespeare's portrait of a scheming Lady Macbeth sounds as if it is considerably more historically accurate than those of either Duncan or Macbeth.

Lulach lived at Lochaber. He may have been Macbeth's tanaise but in the light of his unprepossessing nickname it was probably the ambitious Gruoch who organised his enkinging at Scone when the news of her husband's death came through. Although not so witless as to be incapable of fathering children, the unfortunate Lulach was clearly blessed with neither his mother's guile nor his step- father's prowess. After a reign of only four months King Malcolm did away with him 'by strategy' at Essie in Strathbogie. Any realistic hope that Scotland would be ruled by a purely Celtic monarchy died with him. His son Maelsnectai retired to a monastery in about 1078. His daughter's descendants were mormaers of Moray and married with the MacDonalds and the issue of Duncan II.

The redoubtable Alnwick Castle in Northumberland, the home of the Percy family since Norman times, was a key stronghold on the Anglo-Scottish border. On a wooded ridge overlooking the valley of the Aln where the castle is situated, King Malcolm III and his son Edward were ambushed and killed on 13th November 1093.

MALCOLM III
1058 - 1093

Born: c. 1031. Died: 1093. Marriages: (1) Ingibiorg, daughter or widow of Thorfin, Earl of Orkney; (2) Margaret of England. Children: (1) By Ingibiorg: Duncan, Malcolm, Donald, and a daughter; (2) By Margaret: Alexander, David, Edgar, Edmund, Edward, Matilda and Mary.

During the long reign of Malcolm III Scotland was inexorably drawn towards the mainstream of European culture and politics. This was partly a result of the Norman conquest of England, which involved Malcolm's southern neighbour in the power struggles of northern Europe and led to the gradual northward infiltration of feudal customs. It was also a consequence of Malcolm's second marriage, to Margaret the exiled sister of Edgar Atheling, the Saxon heir to the English throne. Malcolm was known to contemporaries as Ceann Mor, or Canmore. Literally translated, this means Big Head. This most probably refers to the king's imposing physiognomy but it may be a more laudatory epithet, metaphorically signifying the fact that Duncan I's son was regarded as a Great Leader. The first explanation is the more likely as Malcolm's government does not appear all that remarkable.

It is no surprise to find that Malcolm engaged as vigorously as his predecessors in the perennial pastime of most early Scottish kings, making war on England. He did so with no lasting success. Indeed, in the end his ambition proved fatal, for it was while beseiging Alnwick Castle during his fifth venture south that Canmore and his eldest son Edward were ambushed and slain by the English knight Moral. The bleak spot where the king received his mortal wound is marked today by a cross erected in the eighteenth century. The base of an earlier monument can be found in front of it.

Taking advantage of the absence in 1061 of the Northumbrian Earl Tostig, who was on a pilgrimage to Rome, Malcolm made his first sally across the ill-defined southern border. This Machiavellian behaviour was typical of Malcolm's approach to matters of state. In 1066 he supported the losers in the matinee battle at Stamford Bridge, then in 1070 he made another raid on England. Although he failed before the fortress of Bamburgh, such was the ferocity of his rape that there was scarcely a village in southern Scotland without its English slaves. The new master of England was not a man to take such an insult meekly. Two years later William the Conqueror swept north. Although the King of Scots wisely refused to fight, he was forced to accept stringent terms at Abernethy. He promised to be William's man and handed over his eldest son, Duncan, as a hostage. A further cross-border assault in 1079

The keep at Newcastle. Tired of endless raids into northern England, in 1080 William the Conqueror's son, Robert, built an earth and wood castle on a site used by the Romans overlooking the River Tyne. The present stone keep was constructed between 1172 and 1177, during the reign of Henry II.

also ended in defeat for the Scots and was followed by the construction of a new castle on the Tyne by William's son, Robert, and another at Carlisle by William Rufus. For a while these two massive fortresses marked the border between the two nations.

After Rufus had succeeded to his father's throne in 1087 Malcolm again struck when an opponent's back was turned, this time in 1091 when the English king was in Normandy. The raid was brutal, but the Norman revenge more so. Canmore was forced to do homage to William II, as he had done to his father. Malcolm's final, ill-fated expedition took place as a result of Rufus' refusal to accept the king of Scotland at his court.

There is not much evidence to brighten this sketch of Malcolm as a scheming and ruthless man. He seems to have held down his native kingdom with effective government, defeating a rebellion of Lulach's son, Maelsnectai, in 1077. There was no systematic attempt to make Scotland a feudal kingdom, though during his reign some Anglo-Norman barons appear holding land simultaneously in Scotland, England and on the continent. Canmore spoke Gaelic, English and, perhaps surprisingly, some Latin. But he could neither read nor write.

A major reason why Malcolm III is generally granted so favourable place in the gallery of Scottish monarchs is that he married a lady whom less than meticulous medieval hagiography later dubbed a saint. Canmore shines in her reflected light. His first wife was Ingibiorg, the daughter or widow of Thorfin the Mighty, Earl of Orkney. Before her death in 1069 she bore Malcolm four children, the eldest of whom was the son given as a hostage of William I in 1072. The year before Ingibiorg's decease, Malcolm was confronted with four uninvited guests at his court, driven onto Scottish shores by a storm during their passage to the continent. They were Edgar Atheling, the Saxon pretender to the English throne, his mother Agatha and his two sisters, Margaret and Christine. Their kindly treatment in Scotland obviously invited the wrath of the Conqueror. This was fanned to fury when in 1071 Malcolm made Margaret his second wife. The powerful but tactless union was one reason for William's 1072 invasion.

Margaret was a virtuous and devout lady. The chapel she is supposed to have established in Edinburgh Castle can still be seen. Moreover, she had been raised in Hungary and so brought to Scotland's court some of the finer points of current European manners, culture and ceremony. English, rather than Scottish, names were chosen for Malcolm and Margaret's four sons. Alexander, for example, was named after either Alexander the Great or Pope Alexander II. Margaret founded a priory at Dunfermline with monks from Canterbury, but showed especial partiality for native Scottish saints, notably St Andrew. She instituted the Queen's Ferry over the Forth for easier access to his shrine. The queen was not only saintly; she was also probably rather attractive. This would explain Malcolm's politically provocative marriage to her and the wildly exaggerated praise of her biographer, Turgot.

DONALD III
1093 - 1097

Born: c. 1033. Died: c. 1100. Marriage: ?. Children: Bethoc and several
other daughters.

We do not know whom Malcolm III designated his successor. It is most likely that he hoped it would be his son Edward, but the unfortunate young man died a few days after his father as a result of the debacle outside Alnwick. Therefore, the throne of Scotland was for the taking by whoever marshaled his forces most rapidly. The man who did so was Canmore's 60-year-old brother Donald, who had spent most of his life exiled in Ireland and the Western Isles. He seized Edinburgh Castle with the support of Scotland's reactionary Celtic tribesmen and drove south Malcolm's sons by Margaret (who had died of the proverbial broken heart shortly after her husband) and the few English who had gathered at the court.

Virtually nothing is known of Donald III. Even the descriptive epithet by which he is known — Ban or Bane, meaning white — is obscure. Had his hair turned silvery with age? Was he pale skinned? Or did the nickname refer to still flaxen locks? Whatever his colouring, it didn't help him retain power for long. His nephew, Duncan, marched north with the support of William Rufus and deposed Donald Ban in 1094. The wily old king was not quite finished yet. He allied with Duncan II's half-brother, Edmund, whom he probably designated his tanaise, and won back his kingdom. He then managed to cling onto the crown for a further three years, governing the land north of the Forth-Clyde line, but leaving the southern part to Edmund. However, in 1097 another of Malcolm's sons, Edgar, also backed by Rufus, drove Donald out for good. The ageing refugee was captured in 1097, blinded by Edgar and imprisoned for life. His final resting place was Iona, alongside numerous royal predecessors.

DUNCAN II
1094

Born: 1060. Died: 1094. Marriage: Ethreda. Children: William.

Prince Duncan had been sent south to the English court in 1072 as a hostage to William the Conqueror, guaranteeing the continued good behaviour of

Dunvegan Castle on the Isle of Skye, the headquarters of the MacLeods since the thirteenth century. During the reign of King Edgar (1097-1107) Skye and the other Western Isles had become untenable and were ceded to Magnus Barelegs, King of Norway.

Malcolm Canmore. In the light of subsequent events Duncan was fortunate to be alive on the death of his father 21 years later. When told of Canmore's vicious attack over the border in 1079 the Conqueror must have been sorely tempted to punish the Scottish king by executing his eldest son.

But William was more clement (or politic) than might have been expected, and in 1094 this gave Duncan the chance to take his father's kingdom for himself. He overthrew Donald Ban with English support (see the previous reign) and presumably had himself proclaimed king. After his long exile he was seen as more English than Scottish and later in the year he was slain at Mondynes by Mormaer Malpei, governor of that most xenophobic and unruly of provinces, the Mearns. During his brief reign he issued the first extant Scottish royal charter. Although Duncan's descendants pressed their claim to the Scottish throne for several generations, they met with even less success than their luckless forbear.

EDMUND
1094 - 1097 (joint monarch with Donald III)

Born: ?. Died: c. 1100. Marriage: ? No children.

Edmund was one of the many sons born to Malcolm Canmore and his second wife, Margaret. In 1094 he sided with his uncle, Donald Ban, to replace his half-brother, Duncan II, on the Scottish throne. Duncan's English connections, no doubt given tangible form in the shape of mailed knights from the south, had already led to his authority being heavily curbed by a nationalistic rebellion, so that when Edmund and Donald III launched their coup late in 1094 they found themselves riding a substantial wave of anti-Anglo-Norman sentiment.

With Duncan out of the way, Edmund and his elderly relative divided the kingdom between them, Donald taking the northern part, Edmund the south. But William Rufus could not tolerate a potentially hostile northern flank. Together with Edgar Atheling, in 1097 he backed another of Malcolm Canmore's sons, Edgar, in his successful bid to seize the Scottish throne. Donald Ban was eventually captured and cruelly incapacitated, either at Edgar's instigation or that of his brother David. (It is said that, as a final gesture of revenge, Donald Ban had sufficient strength left in his old age to throttle David's elder son.) Edmund retired to the calm and security of an English monastery, no doubt believing there was a greater certainty in the life to come than in the precarious business of trying to govern eleventh-century Scotland.

EDGAR
1097 - 1107

Born: c. 1074. Died: 1107. Unmarried.

In striking contrast to the lusty warriors whom Scotland was accustomed to attract to her throne in the early medieval period, Edgar was a sweet-tempered man of peace. His reign provides an interesting object lesson in government: even the most unruly subjects did not necessarily respect a king just because behind his commands lay the threat of a blow. Edgar's gentle personality was obviously attractive, for he was elevated to the kingship by a powerful group of supporters, among whom were his brother Alexander, Edgar Atheling, Constantine Macduff and William, the son of the overthrown Duncan II. This band was backed by the English and represented the most important segments of Scottish society.

Edgar's character owed much to the influence of his saintly mother. Indeed, it was he who bore to her the fatal news of the death of his father and older brother, Edward, at Alnwick in 1093, and it was he who a few days later carried his mother's body through the late November mists to its burial place at Dunfermline. The depth of Edgar's relationship with his mother tempts one to put it forward as a reason for his decision never to marry.

Edgar was the first Scottish king to use sealed writs as a secure and incontestible means of conveying the royal will to his subjects. These Latin documents bear testimony to his good government. He was little interested in the remote Highland areas of his inheritance, for he abandoned Iona and ceded the Western Isles to the Norwegian King Magnus Barelegs (so-called because of his adoption of Highland dress?). Edgar passed most of his time in the comparatively civilised royal residences of Dunfermline and Edinburgh, where he died. He was a benefactor of the church but perhaps wisely did not encourage Anglo-Norman influence into his kingdom. One further rather interesting and touching piece of evidence of Edgar's educated interests has come down to us. As a gesture of goodwill he sent presents to a neighbouring monarch, King Murcertach of Ireland. Among the more customary gifts, such as items of jewellery, he included something much more unusual: a camel. History has not recorded what the bewildered Irish made of this intriguing gesture, nor how long the unfortunate beast survived in the damp western climate. But under Edgar 'the peaceable' there are signs that, around the court at least, Scotland was no longer merely a remote and uncultured backwater of northern Europe.

ALEXANDER I
1107 - 1124

Born: c. 1077. Died: 1124. Marriage: Sibylla. No children

Since none of his older brothers had left legitimate male heirs, in 1107 Alexander inherited the Scottish throne from Edgar. The new king is a somewhat enigmatic figure. To his contemporaries he was known as 'the Fierce' for the ruthless manner in which he quashed a rebellion of the people of Moray. Yet he was also an educated and pious man, who took great interest in matters ecclesiastical, kept a fine court, and tightened the government of the realm.

Alexander's overriding interest was in the church. Not only was this vital institution rather corrupt and backward when he came to the throne, but also its status was uncertain. Was it under the jurisdiction of York or Canterbury, or did it owe allegiance directly to the Pope himself? The question was not settled for many years, but Alexander and his successors were able to use the rivalry between the northern and southern English provinces to maintain the independence of the native church, an arrangement which was clearly both to the advantage both of themselves and the papacy.

Queen Margaret had paid close personal attention to Alexander's education. She had impressed upon her son the importance of well-regulated and up-to-date ecclesiastical affairs. To this end the king employed his mother's favourite, Turgot, to help stamp out heathen customs and the sins of polygamy, simony and immorality which were endemic in the early church. Because of the York-Canterbury rivalry Alexander had great difficulty in getting his fellow reformer consecrated Bishop of St Andrews and in the end the Prior returned to Durham, whence he had originally been drawn by Margaret. Distinct diocesan bishoprics appear at this time, with chapters of regular clergy serving the central churches. Alexander himself brought Augustinian canons to Scone. He also established an Augustinian abbey on the Isle of Inchcolm in the Firth of Forth after finding shelter there from a storm.

Mention in the chronicles of the presence of Arab horses and Turkish arms suggests that Alexander kept a court of some splendour. Unfortunately he was not possessed of a wife capable of matching this magnificence. Queen Sibylla was an ugly and flighty illegitimate daughter of Henry I of England. She died in isolation on the island of Eilean nam Ban (the Island of Women) in Loch Tay. For most of Alexander's reign his authority extended only to the part of his kingdom above the Forth-Clyde line, as the area to the south was governed virtually independently by his brother, David. Alexander's court, therefore, met in the more northerly centres of population: Scone, Perth, Stirling — at which castle the king died in 1124 — and Invergowrie. Key government officials, such

David I (left) and the future Malcolm IV depicted inside a colourful letter 'M' from the charter granted to Kelso Abbey by its founder, King David. Although the portraits cannot be taken as likenesses, they capture David's authority and the youth of his grandson who was only 11 when he succeeded to the Scottish throne.

as constable and chancellor, began to emerge with distinct roles, and several men are recorded holding the office of sheriff. For secular as well as religious purposes, Alexander encouraged the division of his kingdom into parishes and for the first time a Scottish coinage was minted in large quantities.

Despite what resentment Alexander may have felt at his unfortunate choice of consort, throughout his reign he maintained friendly relations with Henry I. In 1114 he fought for Henry in Wales. Later he may well have felt secure enough at home and on his southern flank to go on crusade.

At his death Alexander left a powerful and influential illegitimate son, Malcolm MacHeth, but the Scottish kingdom passed without hindrance to Alexander's capable brother David, already well experienced in the arts of government. The best summary of Alexander's reign is probably provided by the chronicler Fordun:

> A lettered and godly man, very humble and amiable towards the clerics and regulars, but terrible beyond measure to the rest of his subjects.

As Alexander must have known well, it was the churchmen who wrote the history.

DAVID I
1124 - 1153

Born: 1084. Died: 1153. Marriage: Matilda of Huntingdon. Children: David, Henry, Claricia and Hodierna.

The nineteenth-century historian Hume Brown wrote of the reign of David I that 'at no period of its history has Scotland ever stood so high in the scale of nations'. This may well be so, but the king himself — one of the most able ever to rule in Scotland — remains a shadowy figure. We do not know what he looked like, neither do we know much about his personal predilections, apart from the fact that he liked gardening, showing a particular fascination for grafting. He was morally fastidious, especially on questions of marriage, and was eager to improve the standard of dress at court to bring it more into line with common European practice. His senses of justice and duty are attested to by the story that he once forwent a day's hunting (a considerable sacrifice in medieval times) in order to hear the suit of a humble petitioner. The rest of David's attributes can only be guessed at by his actions and the respectful attitude towards him shown by contemporaries.

David came to the Scottish throne a well-connected and experienced governor. He was aged 44 with years of administrative practice in Cumbria and south Lothian, where he had ruled for his brother since at least 1113. His wife Matilda (the name was confusingly popular in the twelfth century) was the daughter of Earl Waltheof of Northumbria and great-granddaughter of Siward. She had also been previously married to the powerful Anglo-Norman baron, Simon de Senlis. With their marriage in 1114 she brought David the earldom of Huntingdon, with its extensive lands in the English Midlands, and a claim to the vast Northumbrian estates. This made David an English baron as well as a Scottish king, a complex double title which was to have far-reaching consequences in years to come.

The youngest son of Malcolm Canmore and Queen Margaret devoted his long reign to modernising the realm of Scotland. This meant systematically introducing the feudal system of landholding and allegiance, encouraging a vigorous church, seeing that the administration of the country was as regular and efficient as current conditions would allow, and upholding law and order. The feudal theory was that all land was the king's, who then granted it in return for service and oaths of allegiance to a number of powerful tenants-in-chief. They in turn allocated smaller parcels to sub-tenants, who might further divide their holdings. The majority of the people were landless labourers. Although theory and practice never bore anything but an outline resemblance to each other in a state so diverse and difficult to manage as Scotland, the work of King David brought a degree of cohesion to the kingdom which had previously been lacking. This played a major part in enabling Scotland to resist absorption by England in the succeeding centuries. Since several of his formative years had been spent at the court of Henry I, a number of David's new tenants-in-chief were of Anglo-Norman stock. These included names which were to crop up time and again in Scottish history: the de Balliols, Bruces, Lindsays, Somervilles and FitzAlans (who became the king's stewards and thus acquired the name by which they are more commonly known, the Stewarts). The physical symbol of the feudalism was the motte and bailey castle where a great magnate kept his own petty court.

Royal administration was centred on the king's peripatetic court. It was served by the Chancellor (the principal secretary of state), the Steward (who ran the household), the Constable (responsible for military matters), the Chamberlain (with the crucial task of supervising royal revenue and expenditure), and the chief law officer, the Justiciar. Major decisions were endorsed by a Royal Council, comprising all the leading magnates of the realm. Local administration was in the hands of the barons and the royal sheriffs. Realising that wealth was the key to power, David encouraged trade and commerce by insisting on a uniform system of weights and measures, minting a standard coinage at Berwick and Roxburgh, and establishing a number of royal burghs, such as Stirling, Perth and Dunfermline. These were granted the privilege of foreign trade in return for cash payments to the king. Most of the king's income was still collected in kind. This was his tribute, or 'cain', and could be paid in items as varied as oats, iron, or even seals. Although there is some evidence that the jury system dates from David's reign, most law was administered by the king in person or by his local representatives. This at least ensured a modicum of consistency, if not of justice.

With its virtual monopoly of literacy and learning, the church was a crucial civilising influence. Open-handed and religious by nature, David was not slow to realise this. Although later generations were to complain that his gifts had weakened the state, David gave generously to the church. Houses staffed by the blossoming Cistercian order were founded at Melrose and Kinloss. Augustinian canons appeared at Jedburgh and Holyrood Abbey (dedicated by David to Christ's cross or rood in thanks for a miraculous escape while out hunting). Other regular orders were introduced into Scotland. Bishoprics were restored or delineated for the first time, especially in the north. Some of them were staffed by cosmopolitan Anglo-Norman bishops.

Perhaps this paints too glowing a picture of David's Scotland? His kingdom was far from united, as charters addressed separately to his French, English, Scots, Welsh and Glaswegian subjects reveal. Moreover, he faced two serious rebellions. In 1130 a revolt by Angus Earl of Moray, in league with a bastard son of Alexander I, was bloodily suppressed at Stracathro. Ten years later it was the wayward ecclesiastic Wimund, Bishop of the Isles, who headed a rebellion. He was later forgiven and made Earl of Ross in 1157. And there was always the problem of relations with England.

When David's brother-in-law, Henry I of England, died in 1135 he left his throne to his daughter Matilda (often more conveniently known as Maud). This succession was challenged by Stephen of Blois. Though in 1127 David had promised Henry I to uphold Maud's claim, he was sufficiently politic to realise that the English squabble provided Scotland with an excellent opportunity to extend her border southwards.

When news of Henry I's death reached David he promptly abandoned Maud and marched into northern England, announcing that he took Northumbria and Cumberland (including the powerful fortresses of Newcastle and Carlisle) for King Stephen. There followed months of negotiations, raids and counter-raids. The eventual upshot was a crushing defeat for the Scots by Archbishop Thurstan of York at the Battle of the Standard on 22nd August 1138. When confronted by deadly English archers and a rock-solid phalanx of pikes, the 'bare-bottomed' and undisciplined Glaswegians in David's army had squabbled with his mailed knights. The English, who fought for Queen Maud beneath a ship's mast bedecked with holy banners and topped with a sacred pyx, took good advantage of their foe's disunity and drove them from the field. David had previously slipped quietly away to pursue his ambitions more carefully in future.

Although David is reported once to have wept for Maud, only in 1141 did he briefly support her, and then he narrowly escaped capture at Winchester.

The Battle of the Standard was not a long-term setback for the Scots, for in 1139 Stephen ceded Northumbria to them. So when David died at Carlisle on 24th May 1153 he controlled a well-ordered Scottish kingdom which extended further south than it had ever done in the past, or was ever to do again. Content at having achieved more than could ever have been expected of him, the king slipped away so peacefully that those present were unable to tell the exact moment of his death. If nations need their heroes, then surely Scotland has hers in David I.

MALCOLM IV
1153 - 1165

Born: 1142. Died: 1165. Unmarried.

As David I's two sons had predeceased him, in 1153 the Scottish throne passed to his grandson, Malcolm, the son of Earl Henry who had passed away the previous year (see family tree). The new king was only 11 years old. He died at the age of 23, before he had a chance to make much of a mark on his kingdom. Nevertheless, what evidence we do have suggests that Malcolm was an able young man, who inherited many of his grandfather's talents.

The fair-haired Malcolm IV is known as 'the Maiden' because, for some reason, he took a vow of celibacy. This move did not please his mother, Ada De Warenne, who reportedly contrived to give her son a taste of the pleasures he was forgoing. She seems to have had some limited success because, although Malcolm never married, he probably fathered a bastard son. This act spoils somewhat the exaggerated praise of the chronicler, to whom the young king was an 'earthly angel'.

Like his predecessor, Malcolm was a patron of the church. He founded the abbey of Coupar Angus with monks from Melrose, and endowed the monks of Dunfermline with land in South Queensferry as well as half the blubber taken between the Forth and the Tay. The large number of royal writs issued in so short a reign testifies to continued good government and Malcolm dealt effectively with serious revolts in Galloway, Argyll and Moray. The first occurred in 1160 and was put down by Malcolm with the help of his Norman vassals. This so enraged Fergus, Earl of Galloway, that he rose again, only to be vanquished after the king had made three separate expeditions into the south-west. Fergus ended up a canon at Holyrood. The trouble in Argyll centred around the family of Alexander I's illegitimate son and Somerled, Lord of Argyll. By 1160, however, the pretenders were all safely incarcerated, and Somerled had become a contented courtier, with the nickname 'Sit-by the king'.

England's civil strife closed when the energetic and able Henry II came to the throne in 1154. Malcolm realised that there was little point in contesting Henry's claims with open aggression, so at Chester in 1157 he exchanged the conquests of David I for the Earldom of Huntingdon. He did homage to Henry for his earldom but was careful not to do so for his kingdom. It would have been fatal for Scotland had he acknowledged the English king as his overall feudal superior. Although relations with Henry II were strained at times (for example when Henry built up his northern frontier defences, or when Malcolm made a series of astute continental marriages for his sisters), the two men remained at peace. Quite how Malcolm would have managed to keep his ambitious southern neighbour at bay for much longer, we will never know. But during his lifetime 'the Maiden' showed unusual diplomatic skill.

WILLIAM I
1165 - 1214

Born: 1143. Died: 1214. Marriage: Ermengarde de Beaumont. Children: Alexander, Margaret, Isabel and Marjorie.

King William was 22 when he peacefully succeeded his brother to the throne. Although bullied by the English and harassed by rebellious subjects at home, he managed to hang on to the reigns of Scottish government for the next 49 years. This in itself was a notable achievement, but it is not the reason why he was known as 'the Lion'. Indeed, although a physically strong man (in Gaelic he is dubbed 'the brawny'), his nickname probably refers not to personal characteristics but to his adoption of the lion rampant in his coat of arms.

William was not immune to female charms, as evidenced by his several illegitimate children, but he remained unmarried until 1186. And then he had to wait a further 12 years (by which time he was 56) before his wife, Ermengarde de Beaumont, produced a son, the future Alexander II. By this date the rule of primogeniture appears to have been generally accepted, so the birth of a male heir gave the ageing king much pleasure. As a precaution against possible objection to the boy's succession while still a minor, William held an assembly at Musselburgh in 1201 at which the infant's son's rights were recognised; and on his deathbed the king exacted further promises from his leading barons to the same effect. This obsession with the succession, not unlike that of England's Henry VIII more than 300 years later, makes sense only in the light of William's unrelieved struggles to maintain his royal authority.

William was no innovator but he strengthened and extended the feudal government of his predecessors. Though the population of Scotland at this time

The obverse and reverse of the Great Seal of William I, 'the Lion'. The former suggests a tall, sinewy man, while the latter is a traditional representation of a mailed knight. These seals were the essential authentification of a written royal command. Despite his muscular appearance and aggressive nickname, William was not a particularly warlike monarch.

cannot have been much more than about 300,000, the country's rough terrain and the absence of an even adequate road system made the enforcement of law and order a trying task. Towns always foster the processes of civilisation, and William founded burghs at Ayr, Dumfries, Dundee, Elgin and Inverness. He further extended the network of sheriffs and royal justices, often employing loyal but unpopular Anglo-French officials. Following the innovative example of Henry II in England, law-making assizes were held, and regular royal accounts were kept at the treasury based in Edinburgh castle. The most dangerous resistance to these centralising policies came from Galloway and the northern provinces.

In 1174 Galloway rose under Gilbert, a son of Fergus, Lord of Galloway, who offered his allegiance to Henry II. The rebellion was crushed and after Gilbert's death in 1185 the possibility of further trouble was reduced by the establishment of royal burghs and castles in the area.

The Lion's greatest domestic achievement was in finally bringing the north of Scotland under royal control. The main opposition to this move came from the descendants of Duncan II (the MacWilliams), supported by the earls of Orkney (who also had a remote claim to the Scottish throne) and locals who resented the monarchy's feudal encroachments. William first moved north in 1179, subduing Easter Ross, and building castles at Redcastle on the Black Isle and Dunskeath on the Cromarty Firth. These strongholds enabled him to withstand the revolt of Donald MacWilliam, who in 1187 was slain near Inverness by the loyal Roland of Galloway.

Ten years later William's knights advanced as far as Thurso to overcome Harald Maddadson, Earl of Orkney, and his son, Thorfin, who was taken hostage. When Harald invaded again four years later and mutilated the Bishop of Caithness, William once more vanquished him — and made a horrible example of the captive Thorfin: he was blinded and castrated. This at least ensured that he was unlikely to lead any further revolt and made absolutely certain that his troublesome line would not persist after his death. When told of this punishment, Thorfin's brothers, wishing to continue their enjoyment of some of life's natural pleasures, dropped their pretensions to the Scottish throne. A final assault on the north was made in 1211 by Guthred, son of Donald MacWilliam. But the pretender was betrayed and executed, leaving William at his death undisputed master of a kingdom which ran from the English border to the Pentland Firth.

William did not make the task of extending royal authority in Scotland any easier by a remarkably unsophisticated approach to dealings with England. To his great cost, the Lion found that the roar which might have terrified the peasants of Galloway or Caithness produced little but a wry smile on the face of Henry II.

The Scottish king was obsessed with an unrealistic claim to Northumberland. For the first eight years of his reign his relations with England were tense yet peaceful. But when Henry II's sons rebelled against their father in 1173,

William believed his chance had come. He joined the rebellion, demanding Northumberland as the price of his loyalty. The move proved disastrous. After a weak display of scrappy generalship, William was captured in 1174 and, with his legs ignominiously chained together beneath his horse's belly, taken to meet Henry at Falaise in France. Here he had no option but to accept the Anjevin's humiliating terms: he did homage to Henry for the Kingdom of Scotland — which meant that Scottish barons owed primary allegiance to the King of England — and surrendered into English hands a number of of key castles (such as Edinburgh and Stirling). Although Edinburgh was returned to William's wife on their marriage in 1186, it was only Richard I's desperate need to finance his crusade which prevented Scotland becoming at this early stage a feudal appanage of the English king. By the controversial Quit-claim of Canterbury (1189) Richard the Lion Heart revoked the treaty of Falaise for 10,000 merks, demanding only that William do him homage for the lands he held in England. Fortune had smiled on William. It was to do so once more when, still pursuing his Northumbrian chimera, William was warned in a dream against invading England in the time of Richard's brother, the ruthless King John. Negotiations dragged on throughout John's reign. The two men established a reasonable working relationship, with John as the dominant partner. Nevertheless, when William died he was no nearer extending his kingdom south than he had been almost half a century previously.

The otherwise embarassing Treaty of Falaise brought William one unforseen benefit. One of the terms which he had proclaimed made the Scottish church subordinate to that in England. But under Canterbury or York? The question went to Rome for arbitration. With his authority riding high after the Becket incident, the Pope turned the matter to his own advantage, declaring in the Bull *Super Anxietatibus* (confirmed in 1192) that the Scottish church was under his authority. William now dealt directly with the papacy on the important matter of ecclesiastical appointments. King and Pope were at loggerheads for a while between 1178 and 1182, when Scotland was placed under a brief interdict while a suitable candidate was found for the bishopric of St Andrews. But at least William was dealing with the papacy on the same terms as other European monarchs, rather than having his domestic policy dictated to him from England.

ALEXANDER II
1214 - 1249

Born: 1198. Died: 1249. Marriage: (1) Princess Joan; (2) Marie de Coucy. Children: By Marie de Coucy: Alexander.

Between the eleventh and thirteenth centuries Scotland was blessed with a series of energetic and competent monarchs, none more so than Alexander II. He was, in the words of Matthew Paris, 'a good, upright, pious, and liberal-minded man, justly beloved by all the English as well as his own people'. History has aptly named him 'the Peaceful', although those who challenged his authority at home might not have concurred.

Alexander's first wife, whom he married in 1221, was Joan, daughter of King John and sister of Henry III. As his father had done, Alexander kept the nation waiting a long time for an heir. The future Alexander III was not born until after Joan had died (1238) and Alexander had taken a second wife, Marie de Coucy. In the meantime Robert Bruce the elder, the senior male descendant of David I, had been recognised as next in line to the throne. It is worthy of note that even as late as the mid-thirteenth century the enthronement of a Scottish monarch was not officially given the prestigious blessing of the church. When Alexander sought papal authority to rectify the situation, Henry III jealously opposed him, unwilling to see his northern neighbour given exactly the same shielding sanctity as himself.

Although Alexander has a reputation as a law-giver, he is more accurately described as a collector and codifier of laws. The compilation known as the *Regiam Majestatem*, which dates from his reign, probably owed much to royal encouragement. In other matters of government he followed the well-tried policies of his predecessors, striving remorselessly to stamp out lawlessness and bring the more remote corners of his kingdom into line.

The 16-year-old king met the first serious challenge to his authority almost as soon as he came to the throne. Predictably, it was the tiresome descendants of Duncan II who tried their luck, again without success: Alexander had the severed heads of the rebel leaders brought to him at court, where they were displayed as a gory object lesson for those who might harbour similar disloyal ambitions. In 1221 he moved against the north-west, one of the few regions of modern Scotland which still remained beyond the reach of the House of Dunkeld's royal officers. Part of Atholl and Kintyre was subjugated and a castle constructed at Tarbert. Then Alexander's attention was drawn north for a second time by trouble in Caithness. Once more it was the region's bishop who suffered. To the rebels he was an obvious personification of growing royal

The Great Seal of Alexander II (1214-1249), one of Scotland's most able monarchs. Although known as 'The Peaceful', Alexander was merciless in his treatment of those who threatened his authority; the last representatives of the MacWilliam pretenders to the Scottish throne were killed by his soldiers in 1228.

authority, and they burned him to death. Alexander the Peaceful punished the perpetrators of the crime by ordering each to lose a hand and a foot. But the northern Scots were slow to learn. It took one more rebellion before they finally grasped the futility of crossing the king. They made a final attempt to put a MacWilliam on the throne in 1228-30. It failed, and the last surviving member of the family, an infant girl, had her brains dashed out against the market cross in Forfar.

In the 1230s the royal hold over the south-west was tightened by subdividing the inheritance of the earls of Galloway. The scheme was enforced by a royal army, supported by Earl Farquhar of Ross. He scattered interfering Irish mercenaries, executing many of them and sending two of their number to Edinburgh, where they were torn asunder by wild horses as an amusing spectacle for the town's citizens. Castles were then built at Kirkcudbright and Wigtown. Towards the end of his reign Alexander renewed his assault on the north-west, where Ewen, Lord of Argyll was in league with the King of Norway. Royal castles were constructed at Dunstaffnage and other strategic places along the coast in preparation for an invasion of the Western Isles. But in 1249 Alexander died of fever at Kerrera, opposite Oban, before he was able to launch his attack.

As his deeds clearly show, Alexander did not follow literally his church's teachings with regard to the way one should treat one's enemies. However, he was careful to display the conventional piety expected of a Christian king. He made a point of employing the eccentric holy man, Adam of Lennox, as his confessor and he supervised church appointments with care. The church was too important an institution for the king to allow it more than token independence. He made this clear by threatening a visiting papal legate. In case the cleric tried to extend ecclesiastical authority into areas the king considered to lie within his own prerogative, Alexander darkly warned him that in Scotland, 'wild men dwell, thirsting for human blood'.

Alexander is seen at his most astute in his dealings with England. For much of his reign he eschewed the vain ambitions and blustering tactics of his father, choosing rather to defend his frontier with diplomacy. The one exception to this occurred in 1215. In 1209 Alexander had done homage to King John for his father's English lands. Though he had received a knighthood from John three years later, he could not resist the temptation to side with the baronial rebellion against their hated lord. The response of the English king was typical. Uttering a threat that is variously reported, but which was to the effect that he would 'drive the red fox cub back into his lair' (Alexander had red hair), John crossed the border in 1215 and burned four Scottish towns to the ground, supposedly setting fire to Berwick with his own hand. Not surprisingly, Alexander's name appears among the list of those present at the signing of Magna Carta later in the year.

After John's death and the intervention of the Pope on the side of Henry III, Alexander sensibly made his peace with England.

A manuscript drawing of the enthronement of the eight-year-old Alexander III at Scone on 13th July 1249. The king went on to enjoy a long and successful reign, during which the king of Norway ceded the Western Isles by the Treaty of Perth (1266). Alexander's children all predeceased him, leaving the succession to his infant granddaughter, Margaret of Norway.

For the rest of the reign relations between the countries centred around two issues. When Henry III felt piqued towards Alexander, as in 1232, he would raise again the issue of England's supposed suzerainty over Scotland. For his part Alexander would respond by raising the hoary question of Northumbria and drawing Henry's attention to an agreement of 1209, by which Alexander's sisters, Margaret and Isabel, were sent to England with a massive dowry of 15,000 merks to marry the sons of King John. (The exact wording of the treaty was unclear and the Scots also conveniently forgot that they had never paid the dowry in full.) No marriages had taken place. In the end the problem was settled amicably in 1237. In return for grants of land in northern England and Cambridgeshire, Alexander gave up his claims to Northumbria and forgot about the dowry. Suitable barons were found who were prepared to take Alexander's sisters off his hands. Interestingly, the Anglo-Scottish border also agreed at this meeting followed very much the same line as it does today. Alexander was nothing if not a realist.

ALEXANDER III
1249 - 1286

Born: 1241. Died: 1286. Marriage: (1) Princess Margaret; (2) Yolande de Dreux. Children: By Princess Margaret: Alexander, David and Margaret.

Alexander III was inaugurated King of Scotland only five days after the death of his father. The ceremony at which the magnates accepted their new lord was still essentially secular. It involved the young lad of eight being set upon the Stone of Scone in the open air, bedecked with a crown of lilies and a mantle, and handed a sceptre as a symbol of his authority. For Alexander the pageant was grander than any previously held and included the reading of an apocryphal royal genealogy, which traced the king's descent back to Scota, the appropriately named daughter of an Egyptian pharaoh. As the great barons and churchmen of the realm stood about the young king in the warm summer sunshine, some may have harboured anxieties about the immediate future of a realm whose stability rested on the life of a single youth. But few of them can have guessed that they were witnessing the end of an era. Alexander was to prove the last in a long line of doughty Scottish kings from the House of Dunkeld. Through resolution, bravery and political guile they had welded together a single Scottish kingdom which, after the tragic death of Alexander 37 years hence, was soon to be fighting for its very existence.

The fact that Alexander's minority passed off without an outbreak of civil war was largely due to the influence of Henry III. The English king had a close paternal interest in Scottish affairs, for in 1251 his 11-year-old daughter Margaret had married Alexander, then aged only 10. The previous day Henry had knighted his future son-in-law. When it was suggested to Alexander that he might do homage to the King of England for his whole inheritance, the canny youth politely refused, stating that he had not come 'to answer such a difficult question, for he had not taken full deliberation on the matter with his nobles'. Nine years later he took the government of the realm into his own hands. The factional squabbling between the powerful Comyn family and the Justiciar Alan Durward was closed, but it had presented an ominous example of what could happen to a medieval state, whose kings were expected to rule as well as reign, when the key central figure was missing.

The next 15 years were happy indeed for Scotland and her king. There was peace with England, and when Henry III was succeeded by Edward I in 1272 Alexander and his queen attended the coronation as honoured guests. Alexander was quite content to do homage to Edward for his English lands, but when the Bishop of Norwich chipped in with an unscripted suggestion that Scotland too might be held from the King of England, Alexander coolly rebuked him: 'to homage for my kingdom of Scotland no one has right except God alone, nor do I hold it except of God alone.' And there the matter rested — for the moment.

The well-established system of sheriffs, constables, justiciars and justices-in-ayre, backed when necessary by the stout stone walls of the royal castles or the mailed knights of the barons, ensured that progress towards order and internal peace was maintained. The king's income rose to about £5500 and household accounts, which record an annual expenditure on wine of more than £400 as well as £16 on gambling, suggest that the atmosphere at court was a merry one. In this the queen played her part. Although the chronicles stuffily record her as being 'a woman of great beauty, chastity and humility', a story has come down to us which shows her to be a lady of spunk and humour.

One day she was walking beside the Tay with a group of courtiers, among whom was a singularly pompous squire. Tiring of his bumptiousness, as he stopped at the bank to take a drink, Margaret pushed him into the river. Alas! the family's ill-luck turned the innocent prank into a sick joke. The young man was carried away by the current and drowned. The queen herself died in 1275 at the age of only 35 and fate treated her offspring equally harshly. Her elder son, Alexander, died in 1284. His brother, David, had passed away three years previously. Two years later he was followed to the grave by his sister, Margaret, who had married Eric II of Norway in 1281. By the close of 1284 the only remaining descendant of Alexander III was another Margaret (the name was as popular in the thirteenth century as Matilda had been in the twelfth), the bereaved King of Norway's baby daughter.

Alexander III's dealings with Norway had not always been amicable. For some time the Scots had hankered after the Western Isles, which they felt would form a logical extension to their kingdom. After a savage Scottish raid on Skye in 1262, Haakon, King of Norway, decided to settle the issue once and for all. Rather late in the following year he assembled a massive invasion force of some 200 ships and 15,000 men. His army was weakened by autumn gales and unwise strategy, which at one time involved dragging 40 vessels overland into Loch Lomond. Finally, in a running fight up and down the beach at Largs between the hulks of wrecked merchantmen, his depleted host was driven off by Alexander Stewart. The battle proved decisive. Haakon retired to Arran, then to Orkney where he died in December. Troops loyal to the King of Scots subsequently mopped up resistance in Caithness, Skye and the kingdom of Man. The status quo was recognised formally by the Treaty of Perth (1266), in which Alexander was given Man and the Isles for 4000 merks and an annual payment of 100 merks to the King of Norway. Of the present Scottish kingdom, only Orkney and Shetland now remained outside the king's control.

When Alexander heard of the death of his heir in 1284, he knew that he had to remarry at once. The next year he was presented with Yolande, the delightful young daughter of the Count of Dreux. That the middle-aged king found her attractive is incontestible, for it was in pursuit of her pleasures that he met his tragic end.

On the evening of 19th March 1286 Alexander was present at a routine council meeting in Edinburgh castle. When business was over, no doubt fired by a goblet or two of French wine, the king decided to travel through the dark and tempestuous night to lie with his alluring young wife across the Forth in Dunfermline Palace. He made his way safely through the rain down the slippery castle rock and over the stormy firth. But on the northern shore his luck ran out. Riding alone along a dangerous path, he was thrown from his horse and killed. Distraught courtiers found his body in the morning. This sad and avoidable death of one of Scotland's noblest monarchs ushered in a long age of woe.

MARGARET
1286 - 1290

Born: 1283. Died: 1290. Unmarried

Shortly after being told of her husband's death, Queen Yolande announced herself pregnant. This may have been true; it was more likely a phantom pregnancy, a hysterical reaction to the unhappy news she had received shortly before. Whatever her state, within a few months it was clear that she would produce no heir. This left 'The Maid of Norway', Alexander's one surviving grandchild by his first wife, in line for the throne. Margaret was a child of three. Her mother had died in 1283 shortly after giving birth; her father was the 16-year-old King of Norway. All this made the situation in Scotland desperate: not only was Alexander's successor a mere child, and a female one at that, but she was hundreds of miles away across the North Sea.

A group of six guardians took control of the kingdom. In vain they struggled to control the disputing factions which gathered around the leading families. Both the Bruces and the Balliols, for example, claimed descent from David I and prepared to support their ambitions with arms. Civil war loomed as the Bruces seized the royal castles in Wigtown and Dumfries. It was clear that only one man had the authority and power necessary to restore order: Edward I, King of England. But what would be his price?

Edward's terms were set out in two treaties, drawn up at Salisbury in December 1289 and at Birgham the following July. Margaret, 'the Damsel of Scotland', was to succeed to the throne under the custody of Edward. She was also to marry Edward's son. Nevertheless, Scotland was to retain full independence, 'separate and divided from England according to its rightful boundaries, free in itself and without subjection'. This was all very well, but things did not turn out as they had been planned, by the Scots at least. First, Edward's clerks inserted into the agreement reservations which undermined Scottish independence. Edward was already acting in the spirit of these when he seized Man in the summer of 1290. Far worse, the young queen never set foot on Scottish soil. The rough crossing from Norway proved too much for her delicate constitution. She died on board ship, surrounded by the sweetmeats intended to keep her happy on the long voyage. With her death the long line of Dunkeld was at an end.

THE HOUSES OF BALLIOL AND BRUCE
1292-1371

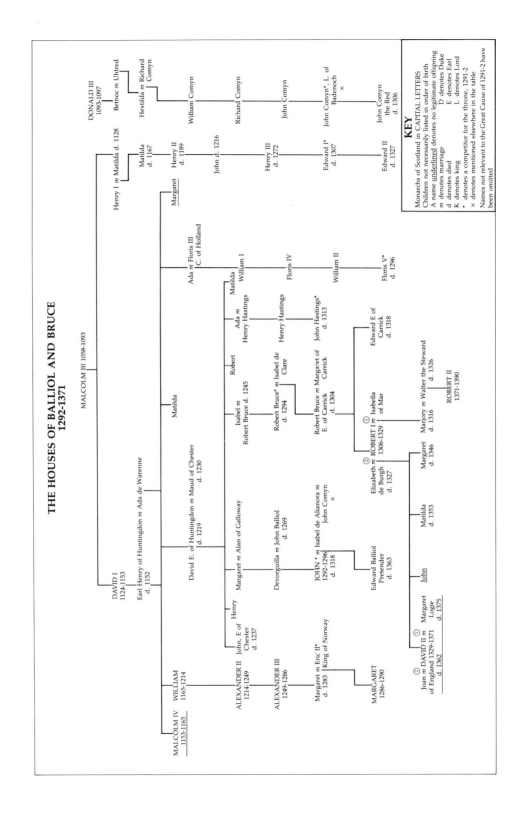

THE HOUSE OF BALLIOL
1290 - 1306

The Balliol family provided only one of Scotland's monarchs. He had the misfortune to be on the throne during most difficult times and his brief, unsuccessful reign was sandwiched between two periods of distressing interregnum.

INTERREGNUM
1290 - 1292

For two years after the death of the 'Maid of Norway' Scotland was a kingdom without a king. It is great credit to the respect for law instilled in the nation by the monarchs of the House of Dunkeld that all those who eventually claimed the throne were prepared to see the matter settled at court rather than by force of arms. But the man who instituted this court, and who stood to gain as much from the proceedings as any of the aspirants, was Edward I, King of England.

Edward was soon styling himself 'Overlord of the land of Scotland'. As the price of his mediation, undertaken according to the strictest legal principles, the future 'Hammer of the Scots' insisted that all those wishing to be considered as a possible successor to Margaret recognise the King of England as their feudal superior. English constables were placed in key Scottish royal castles and Edward made ready forces in case there was trouble.

With preparations thus carefully made, he summoned a court of 104 auditors to Norham where they were to decide the suit, known as the 'Great Cause'.

Originally only two names came forward, John Balliol and Robert Bruce. Both were descended from daughters of David I, Balliol from the eldest, Margaret, and Bruce from the second, Isabel. If strict primogeniture was adhered to, then Balliol's was the better claim. However, Bruce raised two counter-arguments: first, he was the grandson of David, Earl of Huntingdon, not great-grandson as was Balliol's case; secondly, Alexander II had recognised Bruce as his heir before the birth of Alexander III.

Most of the other 'Competitors', who eventually numbered 13 in all, did not seriously aspire to the throne but put forward claims which might be of use at some future date. For example the Hastings family, descended from David's third daughter, Ada, believed that the kingdom should be divided in three. Others based their pleas on descent from David I's sister, King Donald Ban, or various of the royal family's bastard offspring — one each from Alexander II and Henry of Huntingdon, but no less than five from the libidinous William the Lion. Even the Maid's father, Eric II, threw his hat into the ring in a bizarre gesture of reverse inheritance.

After a great show of learning, which involved sounding the opinion of continental universities, the court made up its mind on 6th November 1292. Eleven days later Edward I announced its decision to the world in the Great Hall of Berwick Castle: his liege man, the 43-year-old John Balliol was to be the new monarch of Scotland.

JOHN
1292 - 1296

Born: c. 1250. Died: 1313. Marriage: Isabel de Warenne. Children: Edward and Henry.

Only a king of almost superhuman qualities and backed by much good fortune could have made anything of John's unenviable inheritance. Unfortunately for Scotland, her new monarch was no such man. There is some evidence that he sought to restore the good rule which had been built up by Alexander II and III — he summoned four parliaments and established new sheriffdoms in lawless areas — but the ambitions of Edward I, backed by the disloyalty of thwarted Competitors, ensured that John enjoyed insufficient peace in which to establish himself.

John was enthroned on the Stone of Scone, the last Scottish monarch to receive this privilege in his native land, on St Andrew's Day 1292. The next month he did homage to Edward I at Newcastle, as part of the English court's Christmas festivities. Edward now exploited this unequal relationship to the full. He demanded that complaints against John brought by his Scottish subjects be heard in English courts. When John understandably objected he was threatened with contempt of court and the loss of three of his major castles and towns. Edward also stirred Eric II to reclaim the Western Isles as the Scots had not kept up the payment of 100 merks due to the Norwegian king by the treaty of 1266. The less than patriotic behaviour of families such as the Bruces, thwarted in 1292, did not make John's lot any easier.

Finally, when Edward insisted that John help him with military service against the French King Philip IV, Balliol had had enough. He made a treaty with Philip in October 1295 and assembled his host near Selkirk the following March. If Edward wanted any more from John, then he was going to have to fight for it. This, of course, was just what he wanted. The inexperienced and ill-armed Scottish levies were no match for Edward's battle-hardened professional soldiers, strong in cavalry and skilled in the use of the latest weapon, the deadly longbow. At the end of March Edward sacked Berwick and massacred its inhabitants.

Many great castles surrendered to his call. Then on 27th April the Earl of Surrey and his Scottish allies routed John's forces at the battle of Dunbar. Edinburgh Castle fell, and John surrendered on 11th July.

At a humiliating ceremony at Brechin John had the insignia of royalty — his sceptre, crown, sword and ring — stripped from him. While Edward marched north as far as Elgin on a mission of conquest, John was taken south, first to Hereford then to the Tower of London. He was eventually released in 1299 to spend the rest of his life in exile on his French estates where he died, blind and forgotten, in 1313.

To future generations John was known as 'Toom Tabard' or 'Tyne Tabard' (meaning 'empty' coat), a cruel nickname which suggests that his personality was as unimpressive as his latterday escutcheon. The judgment is a harsh one. Caught between the twin wheels of an ambitious and distinguished soldier, and the disloyalty of many powerful subjects, his cause was well-nigh hopeless from the start.

INTERREGNUM
1296 - 1306

With John Balliol stripped of his royal title and safely out of the way in southern England, Edward I must have believed that it was only a matter of time before he reduced Scotland to the status of a subject province, just as he had done with Wales a few years before. That he failed to do so was due not only to the inspired leadership of certain Scots, among whom Sir William Wallace stands pre-eminent, but also to a remarkable upsurge in Scottish national feeling. Nationalism is a sentiment more associated with modern times than with the middle ages. Fourteenth century nobility, who shared a common international chivalric cultural heritage, in general felt more at home in each other's company than with fellow countrymen from lower down the social scale. What happened in Scotland, therefore, was both unforseen and in many ways unique: threatened with foreign conquest, the Scots forged themselves into a nation.

The story of the interregnum, which lasted from 1296 to the coronation of Robert Bruce 10 years later, is not really part of a history of the Scottish monarchy. Yet so important was it for the future development of the country, not least because it was the fire which tested and hardened the future Robert I,

A late fourteenth-century manuscript illumination showing John Balliol (King John, 1292-1296) doing homage to England's Edward I, 'the Hammer of the Scots'. By ensuring that all 'Competitors' for the throne of Scotland did homage to him before a king was chosen from amongst them, Edward thereby ensured a dangerous feudal superiority over the Scottish kingdom.

that its course needs to be outlined.

Sir William Wallace came from a family of landed gentry. They had already suffered at the hands of the English when they killed his elder brother and wife (or mistress — like so many popular heroes Wallace was as strong in bed as on the battlefield). Early in 1297 Wallace won a reputation for himself as a formidable guerilla leader by slaying the English sheriff of Lanark and scattering the court of the Justiciar Ormsby at Scone. The 'Hammer and Scourge of the English' then built up an effective and disciplined national army which crushed the forces of the Earl of Surrey at Stirling Bridge. The victorious Scots went wild with delight, flaying the body of one of their leading adversaries, Treasurer Cressingham, and cutting his skin into strips for distribution as souvenirs. Wallace made a belt of his.

Edward I was stung into action. He came north himself with a powerful army and smashed Wallace's men at Falkirk on 22nd July 1298. Robert Bruce fought for the English and many of Wallace's noble knights stood snobbishly aloof from the fray. For the next seven years Scotland was in the hands of several guardians, with Edward I making periodic appearances whenever the embers of Scottish resistance threatened once more to flare into flame. Wallace's whereabouts are not clear. He spent some time abroad seeking support for his cause but was back in Scotland by 1305. He was seized at Glasgow on the night of 3rd August — in bed with the inevitable lover — and taken to London. After a show trial in Westminster Hall, he was hanged, cut down while still conscious, carefully disembowelled to keep him alive as long as possible, then beheaded and his body chopped into quarters. His head was displayed on London Bridge, his butchered body on gibbets in Newcastle, Berwick, Stirling and Perth.

Robert Bruce, Earl of Carrick, was in London at the time and saw Wallace's skewered head. One wonders what thoughts it engendered in him. One wonders, too, what was going through the mind of the ageing Edward. Had he finally stamped out a revolt, or unwittingly helped the Scottish cause? For an answer, Edward had only to consider the conflict between his great-grandfather, Henry II, and Thomas Becket. The execution of Wallace had now given Scotland the martyr she needed.

THE HOUSE OF BRUCE
1306 - 1371

Although only two monarchs came from the House of Bruce, at the end of their brief tenure of power Scotland had emerged from her Wars of Independence a free and independent nation once more.

ROBERT I
1306 - 1329

Born: 1274. Died: 1329. Marriage: (1) Isabella of Mar; (2) Elizabeth de Burgh. Children: By Isabella of Mar: Marjory; By Elizabeth de Burgh: David, John, Matilda and Margaret.

Like Francis of Assisi, in his early life Robert Bruce did not give much indication of future greatness. Indeed, when he claimed the throne in 1306, at the age of 32, he could quite rightly have been described as a self-seeking turncoat and sacrilegious murderer. Yet his death 23 years later would cause doughty warriors to weep and tear their clothes in anguish.

Robert Bruce was the grandson of the Competitor of the same name who died in 1295. His son, who does not appear to have been an ambitious man, in turn handed on the family claim and title to his son. The new Earl of Carrick, to put a charitable interpretation on his actions, was torn between his loyalty to his country and his feudal superior, Edward I. Five times he changed sides, often beneath a bewildering cloak of conviction, as in 1297 when he sided with Wallace, declaring: 'No man holds his flesh and blood in hatred, and I am no exception. I must join my own people and the nation in whom I was born.' A few months later he was back with the English.

The first signs that Bruce was coming round for good to the cause in which he was to make his name occurred in 1304, when he made the Bond of Cambuskenneth with Bishop Lamberton of St Andrews, head of the Scottish church. Bruce knew that he was now the obvious natural leader of the Scottish nation and a bid for the throne would stand a better chance if backed by the kirk. Now that Wallace was out of the way, by the autumn of 1305 Robert's plans began to harden. It took an impulsive gesture on his part to bring them into the open. In February 1306 he met John, 'the Red Comyn', one of the country's most powerful magnates, in the Greyfriars church, Dumfries. Though we do not know exactly what passed between them, tempers rose and Bruce stabbed Comyn to death in front of the altar. As the crime was heinous and

King Robert II, the first of the Stewarts, pictured in the Seaton Armorial with his wife Elizabeth Mure. The king's ancestors had been hereditary stewards of the royal household and Robert had built up his power through marriage to Robert the Bruce's daughter, Marjory, and by exercising guardianship over the realm during the absence of David II.

must surely have led to his arrest, Bruce decided to turn it to his advantage and make it the first dramatic gesture in a bid for the throne. He made his way to Scone where he was proclaimed King in a simple ceremony, endorsed by the Countess Isabel, who gave Robert I the traditional blessing of the MacDuffs.

The events of the next few years are too well known to need detailed repetition here. The Scots both high and low rallied round their vigorous new leader who, after initial setbacks, defeated a major English force at Loudoun Hill in 1307. The timely death of Edward I and the accession of his less ambitious son, Edward II, then enabled Robert gradually to make himself master of his kingdom. He used the Scottish parliament to launch an international propaganda campaign, and by 1314 only Berwick and Stirling remained in English hands. A declaration by the commander of Stirling that he would surrender his fortress to the beseigers unless relieved by the English finally galvanised Edward II into action. On 24th June the flower of English chivalry was cut down on the banks of Bannockburn by a Scottish army of half their numbers.

The victory at Bannockburn did not end the fighting, but it gave the Scots the upper hand in a war which dragged on, punctuated with raids, seiges and truces, until the treaty of Edinburgh-Northampton in 1328. This agreement was Robert's crowning triumph, for it gave him Scotland 'free, quit, and entire, without any kind of feudal subjection'. He had saved the nation.

Although much of Robert's reign was taken up with military exploits of Hollywood-style daring, when he could afford the time he worked hard at repairing the ravages of civil war and foreign invasion. Efforts were made to replenish royal finances, encourage the revival of trade, and restore law and order in outlying areas so that to the common people the Bruce became known as 'Good King Robert'.

He also proved a considerable patron of the church and demonstrated genuine Christian remorse for his past misdeeds. Yet his relations with the papacy were often shaky and not until the year before Robert's death did John XXII lift the sentence of excommunication pronounced upon him previously. The explanation to the Pope of the Scottish nation's case for independence, known as the Declaration of Arbroath (1320), stands as the most remarkable statement of nationalism in medieval Europe.

For a while Robert had declared his brother, Edward, to be his heir. When this capable warrior was killed in 1318 while trying to establish himself as High King of Ireland, the succession was handed to the family of Robert's daughter, Marjory, who had married Walter the Steward. However, in 1324 the king finally fathered a legitimate son, the future David II. (Like many medieval monarchs Robert was far more adept at siring bastards than children born on the right side of the blanket.) Thus, at peace with England, reconciled to the Pope, master of an ordered realm and with the succession secured, Robert finally succumbed to an enemy which even his bravery could not outfight: he died of leprosy on 7th June 1329. His heart was cut from his body and taken on crusade as a final gesture of atonement to God for the sins of his youth. But his people had forgiven him long before.

DAVID II
1329 - 1371

Born: 1324. Died: 1371. Marriage: (1) Joan of England; (2) Margaret Logie. No children.

The reputation of a Scottish monarch all too often depended not upon his own abilities but upon those of his English counterpart with whom he had to contend. Robert I was fortunate in having to deal with Edward II for much of his reign; David II, on the other hand, had the ill luck to come into his inheritance at the age of five and to rule at the same time as Edward III, one of the most able and distinguished of the Plantagenets. Not unexpectedly, therefore, David was unable to emulate his father's glorious exploits and he is remembered rather unjustly as a relatively inadequate king. He deserves better.

David inherited many of Robert I's characteristics. In his youth he was wilful, inconsistent and unable to resist the charms of a pretty lady. Yet he grew up to be a brave man and a capable governor. At the age of four he was married to Edward III's sister, Joan, a union which proved both loveless and barren. The year after Joan's death in 1362 he married his mistress, Dame Margaret Logie, a widow already possessed of a child by her first marriage. She was unable to provide David with a similar blessing — or, more likely, it was the king whose fertility was in doubt. Anyway, when David sought to divorce her in order to try his progenital luck with yet another mistress, Agnes of Dunbar, Margaret frustrated him by appealing to Rome. Before the matter was settled David died suddenly at the age of 46, heirless to the last.

By accident, rather than by choice, David was one of Scotland's more cosmopolitan monarchs. His reign divides naturally into three parts. Between the first two of these he was a youthful exile in France (1334-1341); 11 of his adult years (1346-1357) were spent in comfortable captivity in England. A young man brought up steeped in the international chivalric tradition and who had spent almost half his life outside Scotland should not be condemned too roundly if he did not always share the narrow patriotism of his fellow countrymen.

Edward III regarded Robert I's diplomatic victory of Edinburgh-Northampton with disdain. Nevertheless, he astutely waited until the Scots had paid the £20,000 'contribution to peace' due to England by the terms of the treaty, then supported Edward Balliol, the forceful son of Scotland's King John, in his attempt to recover what he saw as his rightful inheritance. Meanwhile, David II had been annointed King in a grand ceremony at Scone Abbey, the first Scottish monarch to be crowned with this symbol of official papal approval. Three years later the king was in exile at the mighty fortress of Chateau Gaillard in France. After the defeat of David's forces at Dupplin Moor, Edward Balliol had ruled for three months as King Edward of Scotland before being driven south again. This had provoked Edward III into intervening in person and in 1333 he had smashed the Scots at Halidon Hill, forcing their young king to seek safety abroad.

The Second War of Independence was continued in David's absence. With Edward III increasingly preoccupied with affairs on the continent, by 1341 it was felt safe to invite the king back from his rather enjoyable life of jousting and feasting in France. The teenage David's second reign lasted only five years. After the French had asked the Scots for assistance in their war with Edward III, David's forces were defeated at Neville's Cross in 1346 and he was taken prisoner. David had fought well. Despite an arrow wound in the face, he had struck out two of his captor's teeth before succumbing. Such valour was not shown by Robert the Steward who, in the sneering words of an English chronicler, had 'led off the dance, leaving David to caper as he wished'. In the light of this, David's later reluctance to accept Robert as his successor is hardly surprising.

The Steward exercised a rather weak guardianship over the kingdom until at the Treaty of Berwick in 1357 terms were arranged for David's release from English captivity. Scotland was to pay the gigantic sum of 100,000 merks in 10 instalments and to provide 23 important hostages until the sum was paid.

Only now that the land was at peace and he was adult in judgment are we afforded a true insight into David's abilities as a king. Edward III was kept at bay with spasmodic payments of the ransom money and tempting hints of the Scottish succession for himself or his family should David die without producing a son. Yet never once did David do homage to Edward for Scotland, and he handed on a kingdom as free and independent as that which he had inherited from his illustrious father.

Despite the ravages of the Black Death and the depredations of war, which at one time had given rise to incidents of cannibalism, the economy recovered, enabling David to build up a stronger financial position than any other medieval Scottish monarch. The exchequer was regularly audited and an effective royal civil service developed under the king's watchful eye. Overmighty subjects lived in dread of a king who did not hesitate to punish them harshly if they stepped out of line — even Robert the Steward was thrown into prison for a while for offending Queen Margaret. Justice was firm but fair. The second and last king from the House of Bruce, although not loved as his father had been, in the end showed that he could serve his country well.

ORKNEY
(acquired by Scotland
in 1472)

SHETLAND
(as Orkney)

Map 3
STEWART SCOTLAND

Pentland Firth

CAITHNESS

Stornoway
Lewis

SUTHERLAND

Carbisdale ✕

Moray Firth

ROSS

Elgin

Peterhead

Skye

Inverness ✕ Culloden
Spey

Eilean Donan
Glenshiel

Fort Augustus
Ruthven Barracks

BADENOCH

Dee

Aberdeen

Eriskay

Braemar

THE
HEBRIDES

Arisaig
• Glenfinnan

✕ Cromdale

Dunnottar

✕ Inverlochy
Fort William

Blair
ATHOLL

✕ Killiecrankie

Montrose

Glencoe

Tay

ANGUS

Mull

Iona

Oban

ARGYLL
Inverary

Scone

Ruthven
Perth

Dundee

Firth of Tay

St. Andrews

✕ Sheriffmuir

Loch
Leven

Loch
Lomond

Stirling

✕ Sauchieburn

Dumbarton

Falkirk ✕

✕ Drumclog

Langside ✕

Rothesay

Glasgow

Bothwell Br.

Dunfermline

Falkland

Firth of Forth

Isle of May

Tantallon

✕ Dunbar

Linlithgow

Leith

Edinburgh

✕ Prestonpans
Pinkie

LOTHIAN

Berwick

Arran

Firth
of
Clyde

Kilmarnock

Ayr

✕ Airds Moss

Clyde

Tweed

Melrose

Kelso

✕ Flodden

Philiphaugh ✕

Dryburgh

Roxburgh

Ancrum Moor

Jedburgh

CARRICK

Hermitage

THE BORDER

✕ Otterburn

Arkinholm

Dumfries

Castle
Douglas

Lochmaben

✕ Solway Moss

Carlisle

ENGLAND

Solway Firth

■ Castle   ★ Palace

✕ Battle

0   25miles

IRELAND

THE HOUSE OF STEWART
1371 - 1603

Famed for their ill-luck and fated to govern Scotland through the turbulent era of the Reformation, the Stewarts eventually claimed the greatest prize of all, the Crown of England. In so doing, however, they sounded the knell of an independent Scottish nation.

ROBERT II
1371 - 1390

Born: 1316. Died: 1390. Marriage: (1) Elizabeth Mure; (2) Euphemia of Ross. Children: By Elizabeth Mure: John, Walter, Robert, Alexander, Margaret, Marjory, Elizabeth, Isabella and Jean; By Euphemia of Ross: David, Walter, Egidia and Katherine.

In his youth the grandson of Robert the Bruce had won golden opinions. Tall and physically robust, his personality was generous, sprightly, well-mannered and, above all, modest, so that a chronicler reported him to be 'for the innate sweetness of his disposition generally beloved by true-hearted Scotsmen'. Yet the descendants of Robert I do not appear to have worn well. David had died at the age of 46 and his 54-year-old nephew was both physically and mentally past his best when he succeeded him to the throne. Moreover, the ageing king did not look the part. He had 'bleared' eyes, the colour of red silk (sendal). From the start the outlook for the Stewart dynasty was not favourable.

Although later mythology was to credit the Stewarts with a dignified pedigree, the truth was that they were just one among several powerful Scottish baronial groupings. This made it difficult for their contemporaries to hold them in the sort of awe expected of a royal house. The Stewarts originally came from a Breton family which had found favour in early medieval England, then moved to Scotland where for several generations they had held the hereditary position of Royal Stewards. Robert's father, Walter, was the sixth Steward, from which title the dynasty took their name. Robert I had rewarded Walter for his loyalty with the hand of his daughter, Marjory. Robert Stewart was born to Marjory by caesarian section after her death in childbirth following a riding accident. He was at different times in his life proclaimed heir to both Robert I and David II, and during the reign of the latter he had acted as Guardian of the Realm on more than one occasion.

Robert's first marriage was to Elizabeth Mure, but he had to have it cleared by papal dispensation in 1347, for the union contravened the complex and by modern standards illogical 'forbidden degrees of kinship'. Whether or not the dispensation legitimised children already born was a point of contention to later generations. After Elizabeth's death Robert married Euphemia of Ross. About this match there were no complaints.

Although the first seven years of Robert's reign were relatively uneventful, the government machine which had been streamlined and serviced by his predecessor was allowed gradually to wind down. Rival magnates, like the MacDonalds in the Highlands and the Douglases on the borders, were fobbed off with honours and payments. Crimes went unpunished. The royal income fell as the precedent of direct taxation (established by David II) was allowed to lapse and customs revenue was siphoned off into the pockets of barons and officials. The Scottish parliament, now a regular and powerful unicameral institution comprising representatives from the three estates of clergy, nobility and townspeople, did not have the executive power to intervene.

Scotland was fortunate that at this time no English king had either the inclination nor sufficient backing from his people to take advantage of Scottish weakness. There had been no important fighting since 1356. With the exception of some maritime hostilities and a brief but destructive incursion by Richard II in 1385, conflict between the two nations was largely reduced to chivalric cross-border contests, such as the romantic moonlight fight between the Douglases and the Percys at Otterburn in 1388.

After 13 years of feeble government, Robert II acknowledged his own ineffectiveness and handed over authority to his eldest son John, Earl of Carrick. Only four years later an unfortunate kick from an unruly horse rendered John scarcely more competent than his flaccid father. The baton of power was handed on once more, this time to another of Robert's sons, the ambitious Earl of Fife. During the reign of Robert II it was complained that Scotland was 'nocht governit' — it did not look as if the situation would improve when his incapacitated elder son came into his inheritance on 19th April 1390.

Robert the 3
Began his Rayne
1390
Maryid Anabell
Drummond
dochter of Listrbhall

Robert III, seen here with his wife Annabella Drummond, was a miserable depressive who had been crippled by a horse's kick before he came to the throne. Acutely aware of his own shortcomings, which led to widespread lawlessness throughout the country, he asked to be buried in a dunghill.

ROBERT III
1390 - 1406

Born: 1337. Died: 1406. Marriage: Annabella Drummond. Children:
David, Robert, James, Margaret, Mary, Elizabeth and Egidia.

John, Earl of Carrick and eldest son of King Robert II refused to be crowned in his own name. Judging from ominous precedent in Scotland, England and France, he believed the appellation boded ill for its holder. Besides, the name Robert invoked memories of the valiant Bruce and sidestepped the tricky issue of whether the king would call himself John I or II. To call himself John II would be to recognise the Balliol claim to the crown and undermine that of the Stewarts, who were descended from the Bruces. As it was, Robert III was given the nickname 'John Faranyeir', meaning John of yester-year, recalling both his baptismal name and the embarrassing fact that he was not, at the age of 50, the man he used to be.

By the time he came to the throne in 1390 Robert III was by all reports an invalid and a depressive. In one of his blacker moods, when discussing his end with his wife Annabella Drummond, he asked to be buried in a 'midden' or dunghill, beneath the epitaph 'Here lies the worst of kings and the most miserable of men'. If the second part of his statement was true, the first was scarcely less so.

Robert had been declared unfit to govern even before he was crowned. After the coronation, the king's brother Robert (a real one), Earl of Fife, was made Governor of the Realm. From this time forward, apart from a rather pathetic attempt at self-assertiveness between 1393 and 1399, King Robert allowed his kingdom to be governed, or rather misgoverned, without him. The royal finances spiralled into deficit and lawlessness increased. The system known as bastard feudalism, by which vassals attached themselves to their superiors for money rather than land, became widespread. This placed further strain on the king's dwindling income.

One of the most worrying features of the reigns of the first two Stewarts was the widening gap between the Highlands and the Lowlands. Gradually the English-speaking southern part of Scotland was coming to be seen as prosperous and cultured, in marked contrast to the supposedly uncivilised barbarity of the Gaelic-speaking northern regions. In the south feudalism and bonds between kin held society together; in the north the system of clans (a word which literally means offspring) was emerging. The powerful Lords of the Isles, the Macdonalds, now governed what was to all intents and purposes their own separate state. Raids from the Highlands on the Lowlands, led by glorified

THE HOUSE OF STEWART

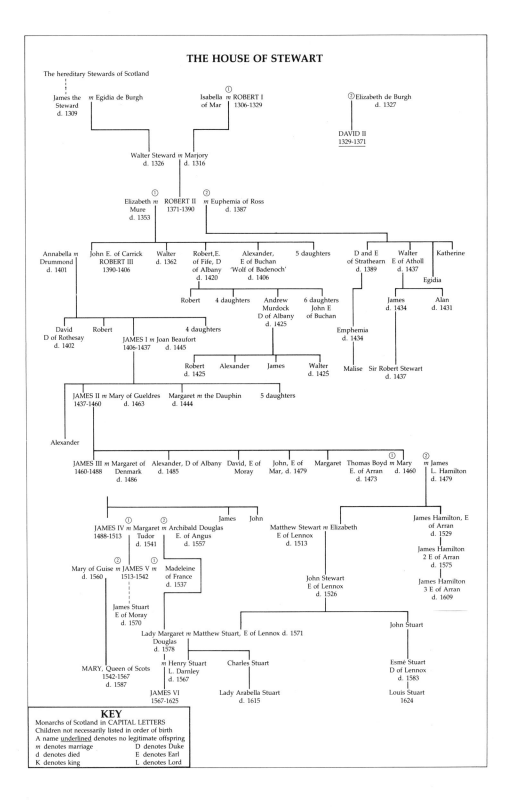

The hereditary Stewards of Scotland

James the Steward d. 1309 *m* Egidia de Burgh

Isabella of Mar *m* ① ROBERT I 1306-1329

② Elizabeth de Burgh d. 1327

DAVID II 1329-1371

Walter Steward *m* Marjory d. 1326 / d. 1316

Elizabeth Mure d. 1353 *m* ① ROBERT II 1371-1390 ② *m* Euphemia of Ross d. 1387

Annabella *m* Drummond d. 1401 / John E. of Carrick ROBERT III 1390-1406 / Walter d. 1362 / Robert, E. of Fife, D of Albany d. 1420 / Alexander, E of Buchan 'Wolf of Badenoch' d. 1406 / 5 daughters / D and E of Strathearn d. 1389 / Walter E of Atholl d. 1437 / Katherine

Egidia

Robert / 4 daughters / Andrew Murdock D of Albany d. 1425 / 6 daughters John E of Buchan / James d. 1434 / Alan d. 1431

David D of Rothesay d. 1402 / Robert / 4 daughters / JAMES I *m* Joan Beaufort 1406-1437 d. 1445 / Emphemia d. 1434

Robert d. 1425 / Alexander / James / Walter d. 1425

Malise / Sir Robert Stewart d. 1437

JAMES II *m* Mary of Gueldres 1437-1460 d. 1463 / Margaret *m* the Dauphin d. 1444 / 5 daughters

Alexander

JAMES III *m* Margaret of Denmark 1460-1488 d. 1486 / Alexander, D of Albany d. 1485 / David, E of Moray / John, E of Mar, d. 1479 / Margaret / Thomas Boyd *m* Mary ① E. of Arran d. 1460 d. 1473 / ② *m* James L. Hamilton d. 1479

James / John

JAMES IV *m* Margaret ① Tudor d. 1541 ② *m* Archibald Douglas E. of Angus d. 1557 1488-1513 / Matthew Stewart *m* Elizabeth E of Lennox d. 1513 / James Hamilton, E of Arran d. 1529

James Hamilton 2 E of Arran d. 1575

Mary of Guise *m* JAMES V *m* ① Madeleine of France d. 1537 ② d. 1560 1513-1542 / John Stewart E of Lennox d. 1526 / James Hamilton 3 E of Arran d. 1609

James Stuart E of Moray d. 1570

Lady Margaret *m* Matthew Stuart, E of Lennox d. 1571 Douglas d. 1578 / John Stuart

m Henry Stuart L. Darnley d. 1567 / Charles Stuart / Esmé Stuart D of Lennox d. 1583

MARY, Queen of Scots 1542-1567 d. 1587

JAMES VI 1567-1625 / Lady Arabella Stuart d. 1615 / Louis Stuart 1624

KEY
Monarchs of Scotland in CAPITAL LETTERS
Children not necessarily listed in order of birth
A name <u>underlined</u> denotes no legitimate offspring

m denotes marriage	D denotes Duke
d denotes died	E denotes Earl
K denotes king	L denotes Lord

bandits such as the king's brother, Alexander (the 'Wolf of Badenoch'), provoked a contemporary to describe the lightly-armed Highland warriors (called caterans) as 'wyld wykkyd Heland-men'. When in 1396 the king witnessed with approval an organised battle to the death between selected men of the Chattan and Kay clans, it must have seemed to those of a more pacific disposition as if the kingdom of Scotland, so painstakingly put together over the centuries, was falling apart.

One serious effort was made to bring the nation to its senses. Clearly a woman of some authority, in 1399 the queen organised a palace coup. The king's elder son, David, was created a duke — the first in Scottish history — and appointed Lieutenant of the Realm. But Robert Earl of Fife, the king's brother was not to be set aside so easily. He too demanded a dukedom (Albany) and when David Duke of Rothesay proved hopeless at his task, Albany had him imprisoned in his castle at Falkland, where the young man died in 1402. The queen too was now dead. Only the ailing king and a seven-year-old boy stood between Albany and the throne.

Although he was painfully slow to do so, by 1406 Robert III had accepted that the situation for his branch of the family was desperate. His one surviving son, Prince James, was secreted on board a merchant ship bound for the safety of France. But even in this, one of the few positive gestures he made, the miserable Robert failed. The vessel was taken by pirates and James was led to the English usurper, Henry IV, who shut the lad up in the Tower of London. When news of what had befallen reached King Robert, 'his spirit forthwith left him, the strength waned from his body, his countenance grew pale, and for grief thereafter he took no food'. A few days later he was dead.

JAMES I
1406 - 1437

Born: 1394. Died: 1437. Marriage: Joan Beaufort. Children: Alexander, James, Margaret, Isabella, Joan, Eleanor, Mary and Annabella.

As the present royal family understands only too well, it is important for monarchs to be seen by their subjects. It was even more so in the days when crowned heads exercised real as well as nominal authority, hence the frustration of the miserable Robert III, whose lameness kept him at home because he could not ride a horse. For the first 18 years of his reign, James I experienced a similar though far more complete lack of contact with the people of Scotland. Not only could he not travel round his kingdom, he was not even able to set foot on it. Until 1424 he was a prisoner of the English.

Before James' release the governorship of the realm was first in the hands of the king's uncle, the Duke of Albany, then Duke Murdoch, who succeeded his octogenarian father in 1420. Albany was an able, popular but devious magnate who believed his quest for the throne would be helped if he alienated as few of his influential potential subjects as possible, even when they perpetrated crimes which cried out for punishment. However, if Albany's unprincipled rule was bad for Scotland, that of his son was a disaster. By 1423 Scotsmen with the true interests of their country at heart were beginning to cast their eyes to the south.

James possessed many of the qualities necessary for the daunting task expected of him. He was strong and athletic, skilled in the popular knightly sports of the day, well educated (speaking several languages) and no mean poet. With a little linguistic dexterity his *Kingis Quair* (King's Book) can still be read with considerable pleasure. In short, James was the sort of young man who today would carry off more than his fair share of prizes at his school's Speech Day. Those who find it hard to reconcile the combination of creative artist and man of action might reflect upon a similar juxtaposition in the person of Winston Churchill.

James' captivity, although humiliating, had not been without its benefits. The young man had gained military experience with Henry V in France, and both at court and from the various strongholds which had held him he observed with interest the relatively sophisticated English governmental system at work. In 1423 he also saw something which impressed him just as strongly — the person of Lady Joan Beaufort. He fell in love with her and she inspired him to write his major poetic work. The couple were married in 1424, shortly after the Treaty of London had set out the terms for the king's release. James pledged to pay the English 60,000 merks for his board and lodging while he had been their captive (a nice way of avoiding the term 'ransom'), and promised to do his best to prevent the Scots from lending any further military assistance to France. That spring James and his bride arrived in Scotland, a country which was equally unfamiliar to both of them.

When James had noted the disorder in which his kingdom lay, he is supposed to have said: 'If God grant me life … I will make the key keep the castle, the bracken bush the cow.' Within days of his arrival, and even before his coronation at Scone, he had diverted his phenomenal energy — previously expended on more innocent pursuits such as throwing the hammer and versifying — into setting the country to rights. His manner was ruthless, even devious and callous at times. But it was effective. In what boiled down to a vigorous coup d'etat he rounded up and executed many overmighty subjects, Murdoch among them. The Governor and two of his sons were beheaded in 1425 as part of a cold-blooded culling of the sprawling Stewart dynasty. Many of the nobility who did not lose their heads had their estates forfeited. In 1428 James moved north and summoned about 50 Highland chiefs (including Alexander, Lord of the Isles) to meet him at Inverness, perhaps for a

An unknown artist's portrait of James I, the first effective monarch from the House of Stewart. Although exiled in England for the first 18 years of his reign, James returned with a vengeance in 1424. Within a few years his ruthless efficiency had once more restored law and order to the country. But his harsh methods were unpopular and he was murdered by his enemies at the age of 43.

parliament, perhaps just for a social get-together. When the unsuspecting clansmen assembled the king had them all arrested and imprisoned. Some were executed. All were humbled. Alexander, whose mother James detained at Inverness until her death, rose in furious rebellion the next year, only to find himself outgeneralled by the king and forced into a demeaning act of submission in the chapel of Holyrood Palace. Such acts of insensitivity might have brought James short-term benefits, but his palpable lack of understanding of Highland culture served to isolate him from his northern subjects and did not bring about the long-term pacification he intended.

Unwilling and unable to trust his immediate feudal inferiors, James extensively employed the three estates of parliament in his quest for a 'firm and sure peace'. The list of measures introduced by him is far too long to be included here — there were 27 in his first parliament alone. Yet an idea of their comprehensiveness can be gathered from the fact that they sought to regulate dress, protect salmon in the closed season, ban the playing of football and encourage the more useful pursuit of archery (James had witnessed the success of English bowmen in France), stop after-hours drinking, and organise fire-fighting and brothel-siting. The royal finances were established on a surer footing by measures which included a ban on the export of bullion, studied forgetfulness when it came to paying the English their due, and ensuring that customs payments went to the crown rather than the purses of the collectors. Attempts to re-establish direct taxation were dropped in the face of widespread popular opposition. Learning was fostered by the patronage of St Andrews, Scotland's first university, which the king had vicariously helped to found in 1412. Although his relations with the papacy were not always smooth, James was a devout churchman. He approved of the burning of heretics and founded his country's last religious house, a colony of Carthusians at Perth.

For much of his reign James' task at home was made easier by the absence of conflict with England, which was preoccupied with the struggle to hang on to its French possessions. In 1428 James renewed the Auld Alliance at the Treaty of Chinon, which provided for 6000 Scots soldiers to enter the service of the French king and planned for the marriage of the dauphin with James' daughter Margaret. The terms of the agreement were not carried out until 1436, the year the Anglo-Scottish truce expired. In the desultory fighting which followed, James lost his beloved seige train in futile assaults on Roxburgh and Berwick, the only major Scottish fortresses remaining in English hands.

Men who attempt revolution single-handed invariably make enemies. James I was no exception. As he prepared to cross the Forth to spend the Christmas of 1436 at Perth, a woman stepped forward shouting: 'An ye pass this water ye shall never return again alive'. James was not the sort of man to heed such groundless prophesies, but this one proved to be true. He was brutally stabbed to death on the night of 20th February 1437. The plot was masterminded by Sir Robert Graham, a knight who bore the king several grudges. Its object was to give the throne to Walter Earl of Atholl, Robert II's younger son by Euphemia of Ross. The conspirators attacked the unguarded king in the Blackfriars' Priory at Perth, scattering and wounding the women who were with him, before finding their master hiding in a drain beneath the floorboards. They believed that they were killing a tyrant. James had certainly been a harsh and acquisitive monarch, but he was God's annointed vassal and his attempts to restore law and order had won him a secure place in the affections of his poorer subjects. No popular uprising followed the murder. The perpetrators were seized and their punishment probably supervised by the queen herself, who had been wounded at the time of her husband's assassination. After three days' horrible torture Walter was indeed crowned, not with gold, but with a burning band of red-hot iron on which were inscribed the words 'The King of Traitors'.

JAMES II
1437 - 1460

Born: 1430. Died: 1460. Marriage: Mary of Gueldres. Children: James, Alexander, David, John, Mary and Margaret.

James II was six when he was told of his father's murder. Over the next few years he experienced kidnap, separation from his mother, and bloody political killings. Furthermore, a large and unsightly red birth-mark covered half his face. It earned him the nickname 'James of the Fiery Face' and made him feel uncomfortable on ceremonial occasions, when he was liable to be stared at. Not surprisingly, therefore, he grew up into a ruthless and devious young man, capable of murder himself when he felt the situation warranted it and probably as attached to the fine seige train he built up as to any human being. As his unfortunate death was to demonstrate, however, even inanimate cannon cannot be trusted completely.

James did not assume control of the government himself until 1449, when he was 19. In the same year he had married Mary of Gueldres, the niece of Philip the Good of Burgundy. The queen was reported to be devout, capable and attractive. Even more important from a Stewart point of view, she was fertile, bearing four sons and two daughters in 11 years of marriage.

The early years of the reign witnessed the sort of squabbling for power which was almost bound to follow upon the sudden death of a monarch whose heir was a minor. The chief protagonists were the burgeoning Douglas family, who held extensive territory in the south-west, stretching from Galloway to Jedburgh. The supporting cast was made up of a host of lesser figures, prominent among whom were Sir William Crichton, Governor of Edinburgh

Castle, Sir Alexander Livingstone, Governor of Stirling Castle, and James Kennedy, Bishop of St Andrews. The details of their frequently murderous wranglings concern us here only when they touch upon the figure of the king, helping to form the policies which he was to follow when he came into his own.

In 1439 James was placed in a trunk by his mother, smuggled out of Edinburgh Castle and taken to Stirling. A few months later the lad was seized in the grounds of his new home and soon found himself back in the custody of the Crichtons in Edinburgh. If that and subsequent occasions on which he was treated as a mere totem were distressing for James, worse was to follow.

During the first years of James' minority the office of Lieutenant-General of Scotland was exercised by the lethargic fifth Earl of Douglas. As his mother was a daughter of Robert III, the earl also had a sound claim to be seen as heir to the throne. When he died in 1439 his title and claim passed to William, the young and headstrong sixth earl. He was just the sort of energetic and meddling youth whom the ambitious Sir William Crichton could do without. So too could the boy's corpulent and oily uncle, James 'the Gross'. Should the youth die before producing an heir, this slippery magnate stood to inherit the Douglas estates.

On 24 November 1440 Earl William and his younger brother David dined with the king in Edinburgh. At the end of the meal the head of a black bull was laid on the table, a sign of impending death. On Crichton's orders, the two Douglases were then promptly seized, given a makeshift trial (at which the 10-year-old king pleaded for their lives), taken outside and beheaded. James might have been upset by the Black Dinner at the time, but he was to remember later that hospitality could prove a useful cover for a coup.

When James II took up the reins of authority himself he pursued many of his father's policies with similar energy. He worked closely with the three estates, who reiterated several of James I's statutes and issued many of their own to help stamp out lawlessness and promote the economic well-being of the country. Considering how the Stewarts had risen to prominence in previous centuries, one of the pronouncements was singularly ironic: it forbade offices of state from being treated as hereditary perquisites. A new coinage was issued. Dress was again regulated (a sign of increasing prosperity and not such a whimsical gesture in an age when attire was supposed to reflect a fixed social order). The system of courts and trials was further tightened up, a move which may have owed more to ecclesiastical initiative than to the king. The church was also responsible for the founding of Glasgow University in 1450. The estates of nobles whose loyalty was in doubt were redistributed or acquired by the crown through a series of acts of annexation and revocation. The aristocracy which remained was not necessarily new but it owed its position to service to the king. By the time of his death, James II was as powerful in his kingdom as any of his predecessors had been.

The Douglases were the last great feudal family to fall. It took the king three civil wars — each one started by himself — to break their power but in the end he succeeded.

After the debacle of 1440 James 'the Gross' and his successor, William, had cleverly rebuilt the family power, so when King James came of age the Douglases were almost as strong as they had ever been. One of the king's first acts was to send the eighth earl on a mission to Rome in 1450-1. Having failed to seize Earl William's lands in his absence, the king resorted to subterfuge. In February 1552 William was given a safe pass to visit the king at Stirling. Not surprisingly the two men started arguing, whereupon James drew a knife and stabbed William in the throat. Courtiers joined in the butchery and one of them split the earl's head open with an axe. The nation was horror stricken at this blatant breach of the rules of hospitality. Although a prepared parliament sided with the king, the Douglases formed a league with the Lord of the Isles and rose to avenge the murder. On this occasion the fighting subsided without either side gaining the upper hand.

Meanwhile affairs in England had been deteriorating fast. Infuriated by the incompetent government of Henry VI, the great families of the realm had divided into factions and the conflict known rather inaccurately as the Wars of the Roses broke out. The Douglases favoured the House of York. James gave unreliable support to King Henry and the Lancastrians. So when the Yorkists fell from power in 1455 James took the opportunity to make another assault on the Douglases. One by one the castles of the south-west were reduced to piles of stone by the formidable royal artillery, which probably included the fine piece known as Mons Meg, on view today in Edinburgh Castle. Douglas power was broken at last at the battle of Arkinholm. Earl James fled to England, one of his brothers lay dead on the battlefield and another was subsequently captured and executed.

Five years later one of the guns which had secured James his kingdom removed him from it. In the summer of 1460 the Scottish king laid seige to Roxburgh in support of Henry VI. When the queen arrived to view the proceedings her husband arranged a special salvo in her honour and supervised the firing himself. But one of the cannon, overcharged with gunpowder, burst upon ignition. A piece of metal shattered the leg of the king who was standing nearby, killing him almost immediately. He was only 29.

JAMES III
1460 - 1488

Born: 1452. Died: 1488. Marriage: Margaret of Denmark. Children: James, James and John.

Both the reign and personality of James III are unusually complex. His inconsistent and artistic character was ill-suited to the task he inherited and for the 28 years of his reign Scotland was beset by lawlessness and inflation, spiced with foreign intervention and seemingly endless baronial discontent.

It used to be thought that James was homosexual. The accusation was put about after his death by his opponents, who did not have the imagination to comprehend his preference for the company of cultured and like-minded 'familiars' over that of uncouth warriors. References to a whore named 'Daesie', together with contemporary exhortations from the church that he should stick to his virtuous (but plain and probably rather dull) wife, Margaret, are sufficient to dispel the rumour. Nevertheless, James did not conform to the conventional image of a king. Physically there was no problem. He was very good looking, with an olive complexion, dark eyes set beneath finely arched eyebrows, and long black hair. What annoyed his subjects, both high born and lowly, was that he would attend only spasmodically to matters of state, particularly those that did not concern diplomacy or financial affairs. Moreover, he seemed deliberately to exclude the baronage from his council, preferring the advice of 'secreit servandis' — a coterie of intellectuals, artists and craftsmen with whom he surrounded himself. He was too clement in questions of justice, frequently permitting offenders to buy remissions rather than punishing them. At a time when the country was beset by rising prices, periodic famines and depressions, his extravagance and covetous hoarding of valuables made him appear insensitive. Indeed, that is just what he was. James may have bemoaned the aristocracy's failure to appreciate the finer things in life; but it in turn rightly criticised his lack of practical awareness. Some historians have treated James III kindly, no doubt sharing his antipathy towards the rugby club mentality of those with whom he was expected to work. But the fact is he was incompetent as a fifteenth-century monarch.

James inherited his throne at the age of eight. Although there was disorder in the Highlands, the first years of the minority passed off quietly in the hands of Bishop Kennedy of St Andrews and the Queen Mother. With her dour husband out of the way, Mary of Gueldres blossomed. She urged the Scottish army to storm Roxburgh in memory of James II, then played an important part in subsequent complex diplomatic negotiations with the

Lancastrians and Yorkists which resulted in the Scots taking possession of Berwick. However, she dented her authority by finding consolation for the loss of her husband in the arms of the dashing Adam Hepburn. A political coup followed the deaths of Mary (1463) and Bishop Kennedy (1465), when the Boyd family seized the teenage king at Linlithgow and took him to Edinburgh. Having shed those who had assisted him in the plot, and engineered a public acknowledgement by the king that what had happened had been in accordance with his wishes, Lord Boyd of Kilmarnock dominated the government until 1469.

Through the energies of the kirk and the ambitions of the Sinclair family, the Orkney and Shetland islands were Scots in all but name. By his marriage to the pious Margaret of Denmark, daughter of King Christian, James began the process by which these northern islands were formally acceded to the kingdom of Scotland in 1472. Like his father, in the year of his marriage (1469), James began to govern the realm in person, although parliament had deemed him capable of doing so four years previously. The Boyds were driven out and James settled down to a period of comparative calm. MacDonald, the fourth Lord of the Isles (who had made a treasonable alliance with Edward IV in 1462) was brought to heel in 1476 and made to surrender his Earldom of Ross. That the north still remained troublesome was due not to MacDonald but to his ambitious illegitimate son, Angus Og.

James was a notable patron of the arts. He collected fine jewellery, supervised the minting of an attractive coinage, acquired a number of classical manuscripts and supported a generation of Scottish poets influenced by the exciting developments of the Renaissance. A delightful altarpiece by Hugo van der Goes, depicting the king and queen at their devotions, survives as testimony to James' good taste in painting. Robert Cochrane, architect and royal favourite, was responsible for the great hall of Stirling Castle and other manifestations of royal magnificence. James was touchy where questions of his prestige were concerned. Although he had no hand in it, he was pleased when the Pope elevated the see of St Andrews to archepiscopal status in 1472 and the king later appointed his protégé William Scheves to the new archdiocese.

The world of diplomacy had always held a fascination for James. Since 1464 England and Scotland had been more or less at peace, a situation which the king of Scots — who had no love for war — had been trying for some time to cement with a marriage alliance. A key element in the projected union was a match between the Princess Margaret, James' sister, and Edward IV's brother-in-law, Earl Rivers. By Christmas 1478 it was clear that the plan could not go ahead. The reason was simple but, for those days, conclusive: Margaret had been having an affair with Lord Crichton and was pregnant.

James' reign now deteriorated into chaos. In 1479, suspicious of the ambitions of his more conventional brothers, the Duke of Albany and the Earl of Mar, and jealous of their popularity, James had them arrested. Albany was taken first but managed to escape. Mar was less fortunate; he bled to death in captivity under suspicious circumstances. Rumour got to work. Sporadic fighting with England grew to full-scale war in 1482. The exiled Albany was hailed as Alexander IV, and an army under Edward IV's brother, Richard of Gloucester, moved north. When James marched to meet it, frustrated barons lynched six of his favourites (Cochrane among them) before leading the king captive back to Edinburgh. Here popular conservatism saved him. Albany conveniently forgot that he was King Alexander and became instead James' closest friend and advisor. Duke Richard, no doubt somewhat bewildered by it all, retired over the border but not before he had secured Berwick for the English. Albany's volte-face was shortlived. He left the country in 1483, teamed up with the exiled Douglas, and made one more attack on his brother. It failed, and he fled to France where he was accidentally killed the next year while watching a tournament.

The king proved incapable of learning from his mistakes. Although the death of Albany and the successive coups in England of Richard III and Henry VII reduced the external threat to his throne, danger lay closer at hand. The common people were angered by his unwillingness to uphold the law, and by the appearance of 'the blak pennyis', a cheap copper coinage. The baronage were frustrated at his reliance, not upon them, but upon his court familiars. Rebellion finally burst out in 1488, led by the thwarted Home family, the Earls of Angus and Argyll and the Bishop of Glasgow. At their head, nominally at least, was the heir to the throne, Prince James. Scotsmen loyal to the king, many of them from the Highlands, obeyed his call to arms. When compromise failed the two sides met not far from Bannockburn in a battle traditionally known as Sauchieburn. The ill-led royal army was cut to pieces, but long before the outcome was apparent James had fled the field. A day or so later his body was found, stabbed to the heart. He had few friends.

JAMES IV
1488 - 1513

Born: 1473. Died: 1513. Marriage: Margaret Tudor. Children: James, Arthur, James, Alexander and two daughters.

Probably because most of his predecessors possessed grave character flaws, by way of contrast James has won almost universal praise. He was able, energetic, outgoing and broad-minded, equally at home squatting round a fire with Highland chiefs as dancing with the glittering ladies of his court. He flirted with Renaissance learning, spoke several languages and was even able to make himself understood in Gaelic, a considerable boon in his dealings with the rebellious clans of the north-west. He looked like a king: tall and muscular, with long red hair. And he was careful to adorn his regal figure with appropriately gorgeous apparel. Above all, however, he knew how to behave like a king: he was his own instinctively brilliant PR man. For the first eight years of his reign he chose to forget his father, in whose tragic demise he had played so unfortunate a part. Then he had the idea of turning James III's death to his own advantage. As a continual reminder of his youthful sin, he had a heavy iron chain fastened round his waist. He wore it, not inside his garments like a hair shirt, but outside so all the world could note (and be suitably impressed by) his penance. When, as time went on, further links were added to accommodate his growing girth James announced that the extra weight was necessary lest he grew accustomed to the discomforture and so forget his past conduct. Visits to popular shrines and a constant harking on about the need for Christendom to unite in a crusade against the encroaching Turk completed the impression of a Christian prince.

'James of the Iron Belt' further supported his kingly image with spectacular physical feats, such as riding from Stirling to Elgin (via Perth and Aberdeen!) in 24 hours. Seeking to impress Margaret Tudor, his future bride, at their first meeting, he took his leave from her by leaping into the saddle without touching the stirrups. (The rash gesture was no doubt intended to indicate the sexual prowess she could expect from her husband after their wedding; it might just as easily have terminated that side of their relationship before it had even begun.) James built palaces at Falkland and Holyrood to display his magnificence. His dazzling court, teeming with poets and musicians, jugglers and acrobats, was the finest Scotland had ever seen. Whenever the king travelled, and he moved about his realm ceaselessly, he scattered largess as he went, earning the respect and affection of everyone, from the barons to the miserable beggars who clung to his horse's harness. His amorous adventures were legion, suggesting a deep-seated insecurity but also further lending credence to him as a vigorous and affectionate man. If James was licentious, vain and extravagant (he once lost £70 in a single night's gambling), it did him little harm. His peccadillos served to make him appear more human in his people's eyes and therefore more lovable. And James needed to be loved.

Although the king in all probability remained a bachelor until the age of 30, he had several serious love affairs. The most intense was with Margaret Drummond, whom he may have married in secret. Their relationship was cruelly severed in 1500 when she and two of her sisters were murdered with a poisoned breakfast of porridge. The jealous perpetrators of the crime were never discovered and for a while James was distraught with grief.

England's Henry VII had for some time been urging a union between the Houses of Tudor and Stewart as a way of cementing a durable peace between their two nations. James eventually agreed. In a wedding which exceeded even his customary profligacy, in 1502 he married the 13-year-old Margaret Tudor.

Although she was grumpy, plain and dumpy, her arrival heralded the first peace (as opposed to a truce) with England since 1328. It was intended to be perpetual. Margaret brought with her a much-needed dowry of £10,000 (English) and provided James with six children, of whom only one survived into adulthood. Even at the time commentators were aware of the marriage's long-term possibilities for the thrones of Scotland and England.

James was 15 when his father was murdered after the Battle of Sauchieburn. As might be expected, the new reign opened with revenge being taken on the old king's supporters and rewards being distributed among the victors. The chief beneficiaries were the Homes and Hepburns, with whom James maintained a close trust throughout his reign. A carefully-worded explanation for what had happened was put about, for the murder of a king — even if he had just 'happinnit to be slane' — was not to be taken lightly. In 1489 the new regime crushed a revolt by the disaffected Lord Forbes. The rebels were treated with a wise combination of firmness and clemency, which helped to prevent the development of a cycle of rebellion and repression. Within two years James was governing on his own — there had scarcely been a formal minority — and at court there mustered a new crop of familiars. Unlike those of the previous reign, however, these were mostly of aristocratic birth and they were seen to wield little political influence. The new king liked to keep affairs tightly in his own grasp. Parliament, managed by the Committee of the Articles, was used to issue the customary statutes to discourage lawlessness, stimulate the economy and ensure that the country was in a sufficient state of preparedness to meet foreign incursion. Musters, or 'wapynschawingis' were to be held at which men and arms could be checked, and the usual exhortations were made for men to forego football and golf in favour of the more useful pursuit of archery. No parliament was summoned after 1509, as the experienced king preferred to rely on more personal organs of government, the council and the court.

James IV showed a lively interest in almost every aspect of his nation's affairs. He built up a navy, the pride of which was the gigantic 'Great Michael', constructed at crippling expense largely from foreign imports, and crewed by 470 sailors. All burghs were ordered to provide a vessel of 20 tons and two new naval dockyards were established. The king maintained the traditional Stewart passion for artillery, a sensible hobby now that gunpowder was revolutionising warfare. Cannon were no longer bought from abroad but cast at Edinburgh. Showing the same practical bent, James patronised a new university foundation at Aberdeen (1512-13), a College of Surgeons (1505-6) — provided with a regular supply of bodies for dissection — and Scotland's first printing press (1507). He backed a law which demanded proper education for the sons of the gentry, and he ruthlessly exploited the kirk, turning it into what was virtually a department of state. He by-passed his father's protégé, Archbishop Scheves of St Andrews, by persuading the Pope to elevate the see of Glasgow into a second archepiscopacy. Alexander, James' eldest illegitimate son, was later made Archibishop of St Andrews, by which means the benefice's extensive revenues were cynically diverted to the crown. As well as involving himself closely in all affairs of state, James dabbled in alchemy, aviation, dentistry and medicine with a breadth of inquisitiveness resembling that of Russia's hero-king, Peter the Great.

For routine law-keeping the royal government expanded the system of roving justice-ayres and the use of the conciliar Session Court in Edinburgh, now acknowledged as the chief city in the kingdom. When something more vigorous was required the king intervened personally, as he did in the celebrated summary justice held at Jedburgh in 1510. The problem of the north-west was less tractable. Although the bandit-lord Angus Og had been murdered by an Irish harper in 1590, during the first 10 years of his reign James had to visit the western Highlands six times in an attempt to force the area to accept his authority. It was only in 1507, when Og's son, Donald Dubh, was safe inside Stirling Castle, that the king could feel that he had achieved his aim. Such was royal authority in the north-west by the end of the reign that a considerable force of Highlanders turned out to fight for the king in his campaign of 1513. Nevertheless, his achievement was a personal rather than a governmental one; after James' death the same patterns of clan-based lawlessness emerged once more.

Initially James' relations with England were tense. There were several periodic outbursts of fighting followed by half-hearted truces. The first of these was made in 1488, only to be broken the next year. Henry VII's support for a plot to kidnap James in 1491 came to nothing, allowing a further truce to be made, this time to last for five years. At about the same time the Scots renewed the fateful Auld Alliance. The partnership was all very well when it meant French aid at times of English invasion but it was little less than an albatross when it involved the Scots in hostilities to support their continental ally. Wishing to try his hand at real war, not just clan-quashing, in 1495 James backed Perkin Warbeck, the plausible pretender to the English crown who claimed to be Richard Duke of York, the younger of the two Princes in the Tower. 'Richard IV' promised to restore Berwick to James for his pains. Perkin was granted the hand of a court beauty in marriage and James crossed the border in search of glory. But the impetuous gallant soon discovered that war, particularly when it involved sieges, was not as much fun as he had imagined it would be. When the Earl of Surrey refused to settle the ownership of Berwick by hand-to-hand conflict with him, the bored and thwarted young king led his men home again. This time a seven-year truce was agreed upon at Ayton. Warbeck was graciously packed off to try his luck elsewhere.

James might have learned his lesson from the Warbeck fiasco. The 1502 treaty, linked to the king's marriage to Henry's daughter, Margaret Tudor, could indeed have inaugurated long years of peace. But treaties are only as durable as the men who make them and Henry VII was not immortal. In 1509 there came to the English throne a man even more vain, insecure and thirsty for

James IV at prayer, from a contemporary Book of Hours. The cultured and vigorous king was the very epitome of a Renaissance prince, with an instinctive flair for publicity. He was known as 'James of the Iron Belt' because of a penitential chain he always wore for having taken part in the rebellion which led to the murder of his father in 1488.

glory than James. War was the sport of kings and Henry VIII was a sportsman. First he threatened the Scots. Then in alliance with the papacy, the Emperor, Venice, and his father-in-law's Spain, Henry invaded France in 1513. James IV faced an impossible dilemma. Which ally should he support, France or England? Wise counsel advised caution: but when Henry VIII rudely brushed aside Scottish overtures by declaring that he 'owned' Scotland, James assembled his army and advanced south.

The Scottish king was a brave fighter but a poor general. His adversary, the now 70-year-old Earl of Surrey, knew his man well. The opposing armies marched to meet each other and, with what seems to us incomprehensible chivalric correctitude, a battle was arranged for 9th September. The Scots took up a strong defensive position on Flodden Edge. James refused to budge from his vantage point before the agreed date, though he was presented with an excellent opportunity of attacking a divided foe as it manouvered to cut off his supplies. The two sides were numerically quite well matched, but the smaller English cannon proved better manned and the bills of their foot soldiers were far more effective than Scottish pikes in the close fighting which followed. Teased into attack by the English bombardment, James led his men down the hill in a furious charge. At the bottom they ran into boggy ground and came to a slippery halt. A bloody fight ensued in which the Scottish king came within feet of the Earl of Surrey (whom he no doubt would have chopped to mincemeat had he reached him), before being struck down. Thousands of others fell with him, including his son Alexander (the Archbishop), nine earls and 13 barons. James' headstrong and confident instincts, which had played so crucial a part in making him such a respected monarch, had in the end proved his undoing. His mutilated body was found the next day lying among the corpses of his subjects who had followed him to the end. Since James had been excommunicated by the Pope for breaking his treaty with England, the remains of one of Scotland's best-loved kings were not even given a Christian burial.

JAMES V
1513 - 1542

Born: 1512. Died: 1542. Marriage: (1) Madeleine of France; (2) Mary of Guise. Children: By Mary of Guise: James, Arthur and Mary.

James V was but a 17-month-old baby when he inherited his father's throne. Although it did not concern him at the time, his coronation in the Chapel Royal at Stirling was a sombre affair, more of a wake for those who had fallen on Flodden Field than a joyful welcoming of a new era. This inauspicious start in some ways set the tone of what was to follow.

The early years of the young king were miserable. He was brought up without any close friends; he had no surviving brothers or sisters (his mother was expecting a child at the time of his father's death, but the new prince soon died), no father and a selfish mother from whom he was forcefully separated for a while at the age of three. His bond to her had already loosened when she remarried with surprising haste the year after his coronation. The young child grew to hate his step-father Archibald Douglas, sixth Earl of Angus, by whom Margaret was soon pregnant again. He held James virtually a prisoner between 1525 and 1528. Although the Queen Mother was officially designated her son's 'tutrix' she was rarely with him for any length of time. She was more concerned with her own political machinations in favour of England than the welfare or education of the Scottish king. As it was, until his seizure by the Douglases at the age of 12, he appears to have been quite well tutored by William Dunbar, who gave him a smattering of Latin and enabled him to become a proficient musician. Thereafter James received little or not formal teaching. To his accomplished Renaissance contemporaries, Henry VIII of England and Francis I of France, he must have appeared something of a northern ignoramus, a situation which did little to help the feelings of insecurity pursuant upon his deprived childhood.

Yet James' character was not without its attractive side. He could be bright and charming, especially to women. Like so many of the Stewarts, he enjoyed a string of doting mistresses, many of whom bore him children; his travels about the kingdom were often relieved by the seduction of some pliant country lass. Auburn hair, fine features and grey eyes set in a fair complexion made him a very handsome man. He partook of food and drink but sparingly, so avoiding the corpulence which usually beset the wealthy in middle age. His concern for justice and order won him the respect of ordinary citizens who were able to live 'quietly and in rest' for much of his reign. He liked to wander about among the meaner of his subjects transparently disguised as a farmer, hearing what they had to say and learning how they lived. This was the popular king of the poor. Wealthier Scots, particularly the barons, saw a rather different figure. To them he was mean, cruel and vindictive. There was scarcely a great family in the realm but felt his antipathy towards them. A strict Act of Revocation (1537/40) gave him an excuse to demand huge sums by way of compensation from those who had encroached upon the royal estates. He took the title of Lord of the Isles to the crown, imprisoned the heads of the country's leading families with impunity, and punished with unnecessary severity those who crossed him. He infuriated the Campbell clan (Earls of Argyll) by setting the MacDonalds against them. The Earls of Bothwell, Crawford and Morton also experienced his vindictiveness. Many others had their lands clipped or forfeited altogether. For the Master of Forbes, brother-in-law of the detested Earl of Angus, he introduced an alien English death by hanging, drawing and quartering — a punishment seen as barbaric in Scotland, accustomed as she was to the gross physical suffering of criminals. The burning of the Master's beautiful sister on Castle Hill in Edinburgh, was deemed just as revolting. In the end 'so sore a dred king' was unable to command the allegiance of his nobles just when he needed it most. Had he been given a better education he might have realised that, fearful though rebellion of the masses might be, that of the aristocracy was worse.

The story of James' minority is one of growing disorder brought on by a factional dispute between an English party led by the dowager Queen Margaret and the Douglases, and a pro-French party headed by Governor Albany, the heir apparent to the throne. He was the son of the traitorous Duke who had fled to France in 1484. Although competent and well-intentioned, Duke John was more French than Scots. He was invited to replace the unacceptable Margaret Tudor in 1513, and visited Scotland three times between 1515 and 1525, before leaving the country for good. After his departure the Douglases won control of the government by a coup and held on to power until James escaped from their clutches in 1528, causing them to flee the kingdom and forfeit their estates. The 16-year-old king then ruled in his own right until his death 14 years later.

As with his predecessors, one of James' prime concerns was the enforcement of the law. Much of the work of his father in this field had already fallen into abeyance. In 1520 a pitched battle ('Clear the Causeway') between the Douglases and their opponents had actually been fought in Edinburgh High Street, so new energy and authority was needed to set the machinery of law enforcement rolling again. James provided this. The justice-ayres were supervised, the borders were quieted in a crushing visitation during 1529-30, and Gavin Dunbar (Archbishop of Glasgow, 1525-47) instigated a gradual reform of the 'Council and Session' court. The council's judicial functions were separated into what became known as the 'College of Justice', whose experienced judges were given salaries (less than they were supposed to be as the king siphoned off into the royal coffers most of the money due to them) paid by a new tax on the church. Parliament met regularly and functioned smoothly, issuing the usual crop of laws to further the well-being of the kingdom. Although Donald Dubh was still in prison, in 1539 the north once again made a nuisance of itself when Donald Gorm of Sleat rose in revolt. Donald was killed besieging Eilean Donan Castle. In 1540 the king used the instance of the rebellion to undertake a luxury circumnavigation of the northern part of his kingdom. Wherever he put ashore obedience was demanded and wrongdoers punished with arrests, executions and forfeitures. Since 1487, when the Pope had undertaken to permit the king a major say in the appointment to wealthy benefices, the Scottish church had become to all intents and purposes a branch of the civil service. James V exploited this position ruthlessly, using the church as an important source of income (raising a new 'Great Tax') and a bulwark of royal authority. Rich positions in the kirk were found for five of the king's bastards. The clergy featured more and more in his council where, after

1532, it is noted that there were almost no earls present.

Royal extravagance made it imperative that the king squeeze as much money as he could from all available sources. In 1528 his income had fallen to about half that of his father and although he soon managed to raise it again to well over the £30,000 figure of the previous reign, he never had enough. He spent a fortune on matters such as a magnificent new crown for himself and building in the flamboyant Renaissance style. His finest palace was at Falkland, where he died. It was rumoured that he left a treasure of 300,000 livres.

In 1521 Albany had renegotiated the Auld Alliance at Rouen. Two totally ineffective military expeditions in the direction of England in the 1520s revealed that Flodden had caused many Scots to have second thoughts about risking all they had merely to assist a foreign power pursue its aggressive ambitions. The partnership seemed to be assuming lopsided proportions: for the Scots an invasion of England meant massive expenditure and serious military risk, a poor exchange for France's irregular presents of gold, arms and a few flashy knights. If anyone was going to succeed in getting a Scottish army over the border again, he had either to be a remarkably persuasive and charismatic figure or the chances of victory (and loot) had to be heavily in favour of the attackers. But for James V the Auld Alliance still held much fascination, particularly as the prospect of a French princess had been dangled before him at Rouen. Such a marriage meant prestige — and a huge dowry. After enjoying for a while the experience of being wooed as one of Europe's most eligible young bachelors, the king crossed to France in 1536. He made the trip to marry Marie de Vendome, if not quite what he had originally been offered, then at least a worthy second best. However, he was so put off by what he saw that he managed to persuade Francis I to let him have his princess after all. Madeleine, Francis's third daughter, was sickly but attractive enough. And she desperately wanted to be a queen. Unfortunately she scarcely lived long enough to enjoy her prize. The 16-year-old bride tragically died only weeks after landing in Scotland. James kept the 100,000 livre dowry, the ships and other valuables which she had brought with her — and married another wealthy French beauty the next year. The blue-eyed Mary of Guise was made of tougher stuff than Madeleine. She brought a dowry (150,000 livres this time), gave James two sons and a daughter, and outlived him by 18 years.

James' reign ended quite suddenly. He had been unwell since a hunting accident in 1537. Then in 1541 and 1542 a series of bitter disappointments threw him into a profound despair from which he never recovered. It was almost as if he willed himself to die. The first blow, a double one, came in April 1541 when he learned of the deaths of both his young sons. A year later, when he summoned the nobility to muster their forces and join him in an attack on England, he was met with a stubborn refusal. For some, disposed to look favourably on the new Protestant religion, taking up arms in support of the Pope was abhorrent. To others, still wary of the lessons of Flodden, the Tweed was a frontier they were not prepared to cross. All of them were united in

'Mary of Guise' by Corneille de Lyon. The second wife of James V, Mary did not come into her own until after her husband's death in 1542. She then played a crucial part in Scottish politics during the minority of her daughter Mary, supporting the Auld Alliance with France against the English party.

loathing King James. They manifested this not in open rebellion, as they had done in the time of his grandfather, James III, but by simply not going to war. After inconclusive fighting earlier in the year, at which the Scots met with some success, the royal army dissolved. James' favourite, Oliver Sinclair, was left to lead a small force, largely recruited by the clergy, into humiliating defeat at Solway Moss on the River Esk. When he heard of the disaster, no doubt with 'Flodden' ringing in his ears, James meandered aimlessly for a while before halting at Falkland and taking to his bed. Shortly after, muttering his untrue but nevertheless oft-quoted prophesy 'It came with a lass and it will pass with a lass', he turned his face to the wall and died.

The first lass in James' remark was Marjorie Bruce, who brought the Scottish crown to the Stewarts. The second was his only surviving child, Princess Mary. The House of Stewart did not end with her. In fact it can be argued that it was through Mary's son, James VI, that the Stewarts made their greatest conquest, the throne of England. Whether that was a victory for Scotland, however, depends on which side of the Tweed one stands.

MARY
1542 - 1567

Born: 1542. Died: 1587. Marriage: (1) Francis II of France; (2) Lord Darnley; (3) Earl of Bothwell. Child : By Lord Darnley: James.

Queen Mary is the most well-known of all Scotland's monarchs. Yet the bald facts of her life hardly suggest that it merits such fame: brought up in France, in 1561 she returned to Scotland, where she rapidly alienated every section of society and was forced to abdicate six years later; she then fled to captivity in England, where she was executed as a traitress at the age of 44. So why has 'Mary Queen of Scots' caught the popular imagination rather than a number of far more plausible candidates?

There is no single explanation for Mary's historical star status. Her appearance and personality, however, make a natural starting point. She was obviously physically very attractive. Her skin was smooth and uncommonly fair, at a time when exposure to the elements gave most of her contemporaries nut brown weather-beaten looks. Her English cousin, Elizabeth I plastered herself with a white make-up (compounded of egg, borax, alum and poppy seed) to achieve the same effect, particularly after she had been disfigured by the ravages of small-pox. Mary had the reddish hair that ran in the Stewart branch of her family. Her eyes were hazel, her face long and rounded, balancing a pointed nose. Although tall, she was not gangly and carried herself with grace and elegance. She rode well and enjoyed athletic pursuits — today she would be called sporty. Her charm and vivacity impressed all who met her, particularly the men for whom she clearly had plenty of sex-appeal.

It was not just Mary's appearance which has made her famous — innumerable attractive queens are now little but names. For a brief while she was a key figure in international politics, a position in which she conducted herself in a manner which bewildered and shocked all who followed her fortunes. The story of murder, lust, ambition and deception, spiced with a heavy pinch of religious passion, set every alehouse in Europe buzzing. To round it all off, Mary contrived to end her life with a theatrical beheading. The woman dubbed a whore by the hysterical Edinburgh mob 20 years previously, died, in the eyes of the faithful at least, a Holy Catholic Martyr. It is of such lives that legends are made.

Mary's short, dramatic reign can be understood only in the context of the events which occured during her minority. Parliament confirmed the heir presumptive, James Hamilton Earl of Arran (see family tree), as Governor. His position was balanced by the presence of the Queen Mother, Mary of Guise at the head of a pro-French faction and the arrival from France in 1543 of Matthew Stuart, Earl of Lennox (see family tree), who because of doubts over Arran's legitimacy was believed by some to have a stronger claim to the succession. Another influential figure was the Cardinal Archbishop of St Andrews, David Beaton, appointed Chancellor in 1543 and a firm ally of France until his murder in 1546 at the instigation of Henry VIII. The English followed up their recent military success with a campaign of diplomacy and bribery which resulted in the Treaty of Greenwich (1543). This ended hostilities and arranged for the marriage of Mary when she reached the age of 11 to Henry's heir, Prince Edward. However, the prospect of domination by England and Henry's failure to ratify the agreement in the time stipulated led to the Scottish Council having second thoughts. Perhaps the Auld Alliance would better suit Scotland's interests after all? Never one to be dallied with, Henry VIII reverted to his customary bullying tactics. These included a campaign of wanton destruction by the Earl of Hertford the next year, known as the 'Rough Wooing'. A total of 243 villages were plundered, seven monasteries destroyed, five market towns burned and four fine abbeys (Dryborough and Kelso among them) razed. Although at Ancrum Moor (1545) the Scots were able to inflict a military reverse on their old enemy, the victory was negated when Arran's forces were crushed on Black Friday (10th September 1547) at the Battle of Pinkie. The Earl of Somerset, Protector of the Realm for the young Edward VI (Henry VIII had died earlier in the year), then proceeded to occupy most of eastern Scotland.

Queen Mary was too young to take much of this in. For her security she was taken to France in August 1548 where she spent the next 13 years of her life under the eyes of her powerful Guise uncles. These must have been happy years for her. As an attractive child of considerable dynastic importance she was spoilt by flattering courtiers and an admiring family. She was well educated, growing up a fluent linguist and an accomplished musician. But she acquired few of the political skills which might have helped her in the tricky task which lay ahead. Back in Scotland her mother was attempting to strengthen the French alliance with diplomacy, backed by gold and 7,000 experienced troops, whose presence became increasingly unwelcome to the Scots after peace with England had been concluded in 1449. Edward VI died in 1553 and though they were free from English ambitions for a while, the Scots now feared that attempts were being made to turn the country into a French satellite. This was given credence in 1554 when Mary of Guise pursuaded Arran to hand over the regency to her. Protestantism, which had been spreading among urban and educated Scots, provided nationalism with an potent ally. The new partnership manifested itself in a group known as the Lords of the Congregation, whose Covenant, drawn up in December 1557, attracted widespread support. The French plan was to marry Queen Mary to the dauphin, Francis, in a way that might one day make Scotland a French province. Before the 15-year-old queen's wedding in 1558 she signed three secret documents giving the French all they needed. Although she was perhaps too young to know what she was doing, this was the first of Mary's numerous political blunders.

The Roman Catholic Church had been ossifying for many years. In Scotland its wealth, corruption and subservience to the crown was drawing hostile comment. The teachings of Martin Luther and John Calvin, which advocated a cleaner, more direct spirituality based upon individual reading of the vernacular Bible, appealed to many seeking religious fulfilment, as well as those who hoped they might gain — as had the English — from a redistribution of church wealth. Although the majority of Scots, particularly outside the towns, remained wedded to the old faith, the advent of militant Protestantism added a new and vital component to the national struggle. It served like a blowlamp to raise the political temperature.

Events moved fast when tension between Mary of Guise and the Lords of the Congregation flared into open warfare in 1559. The Protestant-nationalist rising overthrew the regent and took control of Edinburgh. Newly arrived French troops fortified themselves in Leith ready for a counter-attack. With the death of Henry II in July, Mary Queen of Scots' husband was proclaimed King of France and Scotland, adding the Scottish royal arms to his in a spectacular display of heraldic extravagance. For the Scots this marked the end of the Auld Alliance. Instigating what was in effect a diplomatic revolution they sent to the old foe for help. Elizabeth I had succeeded her sister Mary the previous year and she was already at war with France. Unlike Mary, she was Protestant — she had to be, for it was her mother's marriage to Henry VIII which had brought about England's breach with Rome; in Catholic eyes the daughter of Anne Boleyn was illegitimate and therefore had no claim to the throne. To the French the rightful queen of England was of course Mary, already Queen of Scots and Queen Consort of France.

Mary Queen of Scots at the age of 36, painted in about 1610 by an unknown artist. It is difficult from a picture like this for the modern viewer to understand the magnetic attraction which the young queen exercised, though it was obviously considerable. But charm did not make her a competent monarch and she was deprived of her crown after ruling Scotland for only six years.

Elizabeth's money arrived in Scotland in August, her fleet and soldiers the following year. When the Queen Mother died of dropsy in June 1560 the Guise cause collapsed. The French and English came to an agreement at Edinburgh which forbade all foreigners from taking up posts in Scotland's government. It established rule by a Great Council of the Realm (seven of whose members were to be appointed by Queen Mary and five by parliament), and left the question of religion to be settled by Mary and her husband. Mary refused to ratify the Treaty of Edinburgh. A parliament of dubious constitutionality — it had not been summoned by the monarch — proceeded to make Scotland legally a Protestant country with a new doctrine and a reformed church structure which permitted lay participation. All this need not have concerned Mary overmuch; she was not fired by passionate religious belief. But her life suddenly took an alarming turn for the worse when at Christmas her sickly husband died from a septic ear. She was now no longer the darling of the French court but an expensive left-over from the previous reign. Besides, she had a country of her own to govern. On 19th August 1561, having avoided in the fog English vessels dispatched to intercept her, she landed in Scotland.

Although one might not believe it when looking at Mary's exploits, Scotland was not an especially difficult country to govern. The religious situation, it is agreed, was tricky. But Mary had strong popular support when she arrived and there is no particular reason to suppose that she should not have fared at least as well as her namesake and cousin, Mary I of England, if not as ably as Elizabeth. All that she had to do was take good advice, fulfill the duties expected of her, and remain on good terms with at least some of her more influential subjects. All of these she spectacularly failed to do. Moreover, obsessed with the idea of wining the altogether grander throne of England, she gave the impression of caring little for Scotland or her people.

Much day-to-day government was left to the Council. Deprived of royal leadership, like a cabinet without a prime minister, it inevitably tended to divide into factions, which lessened its authority. Mary remained in her own rooms, accompanied by a resented coterie of favourites comprising several foreigners, such as the secretary Rizzio, the Englishman Fowler and Francisco de Busso. Experienced councillors, headed by Lord James Stewart, Earl of Moray, and Secretary of State William Maitland of Lethington, tended to be ignored: consequently they grew restless. As a Catholic, Mary insisted on retaining the right to have Mass said in her chapels, a concession which provoked some unpopularity. But she did not move against the Protestant kirk, even when the rabble-rousing preacher John Knox overstepped the mark in his personal addresses to her. In 1566 she actually donated £10,000 of her own money to the church and no representative was sent to the third session of the Council of Trent, the driving force behind the Catholic Church's Counter Reformation. A Protestant plot by the Earl of Arran, who was now verging upon insanity, and a revolt by Earl Huntley, aimed more at James Stewart than the queen, both came to nothing. The issue which finally brought matters to a head was Mary's marriage.

As an attractive heiress in her early twenties, whose future husband could — if he played his cards right — expect to be at least her equal in directing Scottish affairs, Mary was one of the two most eligible ladies in Europe. The other was Elizabeth I. The latter never married, although she would dearly have liked to do so. She chose rather to use her marriageability as a powerful diplomatic weapon. Mary showed no such sense of duty. She wanted a man. Many were on offer: there were the kings of Sweden and Denmark, the sons of the Emperor Charles V, the son of Spain's Phillip II (a serious candidate until he went mad), as well as Elizabeth's suggestion of Robert Dudley, and a number of suitable Scotsmen. Whomever Mary chose, the situation would require careful handling in case it fed Scottish xenophobia or domestic resentment among the thwarted parties. As it was, she made a poor choice, selecting Henry Lord Darnley because he was 'the lustiest and best proportionit man that sche had seen'. Furthermore, she believed a union with him would strengthen the Stewart claim to the throne of England (see family tree). The marriage drove Lord James and other Protestant nobles to a revolt which was put down in the hectic 'Chase About Raid'.

It was not long before Mary was estranged from her weak, jealous young husband. Early in 1566 he put himself at the head of a group of nobles (including the Earl of Morton, and the Lords Lindsay and Ruthven) determined to break his wife's circle of favourites. Their target was Rizzio, and perhaps even the queen herself. They entered Mary's appartments on 9th February, threatened her with a pistol and laid hold of the miserable secretary. Mary was six months pregnant at the time, almost certainly by her husband although rumour credited Rizzio with being the unborn child's father. Jabbering for mercy in broken English, he was torn from Mary's skirts and stabbed to death outside the room. Darnley's dagger was left sticking in the corpse. Mary would never forgive him, either for the humiliation, or for endangering her unborn child.

Nevertheless, some sort of reconciliation was effected between husband and wife and the murderers fled to England, from where they were permitted to return the following year. In the meantime, assuring Darnley over and over again that he was the father, Mary gave birth to a son, the future James VI. If Mary was telling the truth and had not yet given Darnley grounds for his wild jealousy, she was soon to do so. Marriage, even though it was to the insipid Darnley, had whetted her sexual appetite. She began an affair with James Hepburn, Earl of Bothwell, whose rugged charms were much more to her taste. Unfair though it might seem to modern eyes, in the seventeenth century the licence permitted to men to slake their desires as they could was not extended to women. Life for Mary, particularly since she was pregnant by her lover, would obviously be much easier if Darnley were out of the way. He had not been near her for months and he had been difficult enough over the paternity of James. This time he was capable of ruining her for ever. Quite how Darnley died and who was directly responsible for the murder remains a mystery. The bare facts are that he was moved to Kirk O'Fields House outside Edinburgh to recover from a bout of syphilis. The house was blown up on the night of 10th February 1567, and Darnley was found strangled in the grounds. Bothwell then promptly divorced the wife he had married the previous year. Acquitted for Darnley's murder at a trial demanded by Lennox (who was prevented from giving evidence by the presence in Edinburgh of large numbers of Bothwell's men), on 15th May Bothwell married Mary. The queen had tried to justify herself with a concocted story of abduction and rape. No-one believed her.

Not surprisingly, Mary's reign now promptly collapsed. She was universally disparaged. The troops she assembled against her opponents deserted. She was taken prisoner, first in Edinburgh then in Loch Leven, where she was forced to abdicate in favour of her son. No longer a monarch of Scotland, the rest of her story does not really lie within the scope of these pages. But for the sake of tidiness it can be recorded that she escaped from captivity, found a surprisingly large body of support, but lost it in battle at Langside in May 1568. She then fled by sea to England. Detained with increasing security by Elizabeth, she spent the rest of her life rediscovering her attachment to the Roman faith while fretting and plotting for her cousin's elusive throne. Finally even the dithering Elizabeth, who never made a decision until was was forced into it, decided that she had had enough. Mary, no longer Queen of Scots, was executed in Fotheringay Castle on 8th February 1587.

It is easy to condemn Mary. But she had not chosen to be a queen. If judgment is needed, then perhaps it should be on the system which can raise to positions of the highest authority persons totally unfitted to bear such responsibility.

JAMES VI
1567 - 1625
(James I of England 1603 - 1625)

Born: 1566. Died: 1625. Marriage: Anne of Denmark. Children: Henry, Charles, Robert, an unnamed son, Elizabeth, Margaret, Mary and Sophia.

The long minorities of Mary and her son James, together with the queen's brief and tragic reign, put Scottish government under greater pressure than at any time since the Wars of Independence. Yet never once did any serious

James VI aged 29, in a portrait attributed to Adrian Vanson. For a long time the reputation of this scholarly but capable monarch was besmirched by English historians who took at its face value the quip that James was 'the wisest fool in Christendom'. Today he is more favourably regarded as an able ruler of both Scotland and, as James I, of England.

opposition arise to the institution of monarchy. In 1567 the Scots removed an incompetent queen but unlike the English, who in 1649 did away with both king and kingship, they retained confidence in the system which Mary had so dramatically failed to operate. Scotland needed her monarchs to counter the centrifugal forces pulling at the state. In a sense the monarchy was Scotland — it had created, nourished and maintained the nation. More than in England, the relationship between the people and the crown was one of partnership. The great achievement of James VI, one of the most competent of the Stewart kings, was to see that partnership restored and strengthened.

Born the year before his mother's abdication, it was 16 years before James VI began to exercise any consistent influence over the government. Predictably enough, the intervening years were peppered with plot, assassination, religious turmoil and civil disorder. Four regents tried their hand at controlling the situation: the Earls of Moray (James Stewart, an illegitimate son of James V) 1567-70; Lennox (Matthew Stewart, the father of Darnley) 1570-1; Mar (John Erskine, the custodian of King James) 1571-2; and Morton (James Douglas, the most able of the quartet) 1572-8 and in control of the administration until 1580. The first two were murdered, the last executed; the third, Mar, died of what were supposed to be natural causes before anyone could get at him.

The power struggle coalesced around two groups, the king's party and the queen's party. The former found support among Lowlanders and the Protestant kirk; the latter, which hoped Mary might divorce Bothwell, reconcile herself to Queen Elizabeth and make a dramatic return to Scotland, were based upon Catholic and Highland interests. Once during Lennox's regency the two sides held almost simultaneous parliaments in Edinburgh. Although there were many attempts to kidnap him, such as that which led to Lennox's death, James remained reasonably secure in Stirling's high castle. Elizabeth, unwilling to support rebels who had overthrown a crowned monarch yet also wary of helping to restore to power someone who claimed the English throne, was content to see the northern kingdom rendered impotent by domestic troubles. She kept a close eye on the situation, intervening every now and again, but showing little liking for James ('a Scottes man') or for a church which could tolerate a preacher who condemned her as an atheist. Under the influence of Andrew Melville and others a Second Book of Discipline was drawn up. This established a Presbyterian system in all but name, eschewing episcopacy and introducing stringent Sabbatarianism. However, there was all the difference in the world between the pronouncements of enthusiasts in Edinburgh and the practices in Highland glens or on the Western Isles. Whatever else there was in Scottish religion at this time, there was not uniformity.

In 1578 James was used to back a short-lived coup by the Earls of Atholl and Argyll, members of the northern pro-Catholic faction. Although only 12 the young king was starting make a mark on politics. Two years later he rode on his first important royal progress. By this time he had come under the influence of Esme Stuart, Seigneur d'Aubigny (see family tree). James became obsessed with this attractive man from the sophisticated French court, whose polish, wit and lightly-worn religious principles contrasted vividly with the court's earnest clerics and dour nobility. Above all, d'Aubigny knew how to flatter. He lavished attention on the impressionable and sensitive boy king. From an early age James craved affection. He would demonstrate his fondness for those who responded to him with open demonstrations of physical tenderness which embarrassed others present. He missed d'Aubigny when he was away and would rush to kiss him on his return. This sort of behaviour was typical of James all his life and has led to his being labelled a homosexual. However, there is no concrete evidence to support the allegation that public petting was followed by more intimate relations in private. As d'Aubigny's star waxed — he was created a Privy Councillor and Duke of Lennox in 1581 — so Morton's waned. Accused of complicity in Darnley's murder, he was executed in 1581. But the Protestant anglophile party was also threatened by Lennox's increasing power. James was forced to make a Negative Confession, renouncing all popery. The next year he was seized while hunting by the Earl of Gowrie (with the tacit backing of Queen Elizabeth) and taken to Ruthven Castle. Here he was compelled to order Lennox from the country. When the Duke died in France a few years later he left his embalmed heart to the young King of Scots. Although separation from Lennox left him bitterly unhappy, the Ruthven raid was the last humiliation of James' childhood. With the help of James Stewart, Earl of Arran (a soldier of fortune who had risen in royal favour) James escaped from Ruthven in 1583. From now on he directed affairs of state himself.

What sort of young man was it who now stepped forward to the centre of the political stage? At the age of 16 he was old before his time. Nine attempts at kidnap had left him fearful and suspicious. Some reports indicate that he never overcame his dread of assassination, wearing thick padded clothes and eyeing carefully all strangers who came into his presence. He disliked soldiering and inherited little of the machismo that marked most of his Stewart predecessors. Yet he was no lounge lizard. Hunting was his great passion; he would frequently infuriate conscientious ministers and secretaries by suddenly taking off for days in the saddle, leaving behind piles of untouched paperwork. His intelligence and perception made him generally an astute judge of character although — as we saw in the case of Lennox — his penchant for attractive male company drew him into demeaning displays of tenderness towards favourites not always worthy of royal favour. The tedium of court etiquette sometimes produced from him the sort of cynical outbursts associated with a man of academic inclinations. 'God's wounds!' he cried on one occasion when pressed by a crowd of fawning English courtiers, 'I will pull down my breeches and they shall see my arse!' James was intelligent and very well educated. His schooling had been carefully supervised by the stern humanist scholar George Buchanan, assisted by the more kindly Peter Young. The daily routine started before breakfast with Greek, then proceeded via Latin and history to music, mathematics, geography, astronomy and public speaking. Complaints by the

English that James had a speech impediment probably arose from their failure to cope with his alien Scots accent. During these early years the king developed a life-long love of books and learning. He built up a fine library to which he contributed with several works of his own authorship. These ranged widely in their subject matter from witchcraft and tobacco to a splendid treatise on kingship, *Basilikon Doron*, marked by its practical balance between a monarch's exalted God-given authority and his duty towards his subjects. There is some controversy about James' physical appearance. Critics say he had a peculiar, 'circular' walk, suggesting that he had suffered from rickets. Other contemporaries describe him as well-built and healthy, making no mention of deformity. He inherited his family's red hair, which turned dark brown in later life. Large, doleful eyes were the main feature of an unhappy face.

James did not govern Scotland with the pen, as he later told his English subjects he was able to do. But neither did he govern with the sword. To control his dangerous inheritance he employed the arts of politics, balancing one group against another and never moving until he was sure that the ground had been carefully prepared beforehand. At first he employed James Stewart, Earl of Arran, as his chief minister, making him Chancellor in 1584. He was followed by the highly competent Sir John Maitland, Secretary (1584), Chancellor (1587), and created Lord Maitland of Thirlestane in 1590 as a reward for his services. With one short break (1592-4) he remained in office until his death in 1590. The king's policy towards the overmighty subjects who had wielded so much power over the last four decades was not to tackle them head on, but gradually to exclude them from his government and allow them sufficient licence to bring about their own downfall. This tactic was successfully used with the northern earls, a group headed by the Earl of Huntly. James was fond of the earl, who was married to one of Lennox's daughters, and the leniency shown towards him stemmed from a blend of policy and affection. After the swaggering young Gordon had been involved with several Catholic plots and with the murder in 1592 of the Earl of Moray, James allied with the kirk to drive him abroad in 1595. After this Roman Catholicism ceased to be a political danger. Subversive ultra-Protestantism was personified in Francis Stewart, Earl of Bothwell, one of James V's illegitimate offspring. His misdeeds included employing witchcraft against James on his trip to Denmark in 1589, and engaging on a number of yobbish attacks on royal residences. He too was driven into exile in 1595, dying in Naples 18 years later. Lesser lawbreakers were dealt with more swiftly. The likelihood of future trouble was lessened by restrictions placed on the size of personal revenues. New men who owed their position and fortune to loyal service gradually replaced the older nobility in the royal council. The canny scholar succeeded where many warriors had failed. James' tactics did not inspire the ballad makers or elevate the king to the status of a national hero. Nevertheless by 1597 factional noble revolts were at an end and the country entered on a long era of domestic peace. The only serious hiccup occurred with the mysterious Gowrie Conspiracy of 1600, which resulted in the brutal murder of the young earl and his brother at Perth. It is not clear whether the king or the Ruthvens instigated the plot, or whether in fact there was a plot at all.

The 'Black Acts' of 1584 had reaffirmed the existence of episcopacy (an institution abhored by the more zealous Presbyterians) and reminded the kirk that it was not a state within a state, but part of a single kingdom beneath king, council and parliament. The result was an oddly mixed church, basically Calvinistic, but with a system of bishops and royal authority superimposed upon it. While he was tackling the northern earls the king was unwilling to alienate Andrew Melville and the leading Presbyterians. An Act of Parliament in 1592 officially recognised that Scotland was a Presbyterian state. Four years later, with the threat from the turbulent nobility behind him, James turned his attention to the church. Like their aristocratic counterparts, militant clerics were overstepping the mark: one fanatical preacher even went as far as to declare that 'all kings are the devil's children'. James skilfully used rumours of a popish plot in 1597 to turn the tables against these mischievous ministers, whose excesses were curbed by an increasingly potent royal authority.

James married at the age of 23. His bride was Anne of Denmark, a pretty Scandinavian blonde who, although not James' equal intellectually, brought to the court vivacity and an interest in the arts which blossomed into good taste over the years. The two were married by proxy. When stormy weather delayed Anne's journey to Scotland, James travelled to Denmark to collect her — an unusually romantic gesture on his part. Much of the king's later life was taken up with matters of government, hunting and dalliance with his favourites, so his relationship with his queen does not seem to have been anything other than what one might expect from an arranged marriage between foreigners. Neither were affections deepened when Anne tactlessly converted to Roman Catholicism. Notwithstanding this, the two got on tolerably well. James fathered eight children (not a bad effort for one supposed to be homosexual), only three of whom survived into adulthood.

Two other women played an important part in James' adult life in Scotland, his mother and Queen Elizabeth. James is sometimes criticised for not caring more closely for Mary. Yet his detachment is hardly surprising, considering her abandonment of him and the constant barrage of abuse heaped upon her by James' childhood tutors. His correspondence with his mother varied from the formal to the affectionate; once he suggested that they should reign together as joint sovereigns. He was genuinely upset at her death, but the sorrow was for what might have been, not for any lost comfort. The relationship between James and Elizabeth was a practical one between two sharp politicians. When James would not fit in with her schemes the queen could upbraid him as 'that false Scots urchin'. For his part, along with many of her own councillors, James continually pressurised her formally to recognise him as her successor. This, partly through vanity and partly for political reasons, she obstinately refused to do. Even on her death bed, when asked if

James was to succeed her she replied with an ambiguous sign. The closest the two kingdoms had come was forming of a league for mutual defence (1586), when James was granted a pension of £4000 a year. He would have liked more, for he was extravagant and found the royal income woefully inadequate for his needs, particularly after his marriage. But he could wait. When Elizabeth died he would no longer need her paltry pension. He would have her crown instead. Elizabeth passed quietly away early in the morning of 24th March 1603. Later in the day, as messengers sped north bearing the joyous news to James, in London the King of Scots was proclaimed King of England and Ireland. Fortune had given James the prize denied to his mother and several illustrious English ancestors: the united crowns of England and Scotland. Henceforward the House of Stewart would be known by the French version of their name, Stuart, and their monarchs would rule the land of their ancestors not from Edinburgh, Perth or Stirling, but from London. The consequences for Scotland were momentous.

THE UNION OF THE CROWNS
OF SCOTLAND AND ENGLAND

Apart from his short Danish jaunt, James VI had never been out of Scotland before his journey to England in the spring of 1603. This second trip abroad thrilled him. He was intoxicated by the wealth, sophistication and clement climate of England. Thus befuddled with happiness he drew up a scheme which he believed would spread among all his subjects the benefits which he now enjoyed: James proposed a full union of England and Scotland to form the single realm of Great Britain.

James, a Scotsman, loved England — why should his Scots subjects not do the same? And the English had welcomed him most warmly as their king — why should they not show the same affection towards his Scottish compatriots? If the memories of centuries of bitter warfare, border raids and racial harassment could have been erased by royal fiat, then James would have succeeded. As it was, his grand proposal provoked bitter hostility in the English parliament and was dropped. Fortune hunters who had come south with their king were scorned as 'northern adjectives' or 'Caledonian bores'. 'They beg our lands, our goods, our lives', complained one Englishman, 'They switch our nobles, and lye with their wives'. A few decades later another southerner was to write of Scotland: 'The aire might be wholesome but for the stinking people that inhabit it.' With such attitudes prevalent even among the educated classes in England, James' dream was certain never to become a reality during his lifetime. The Scots, fearful of being swallowed up by their powerful neighbour, of losing the national identity which they had striven so hard to maintain over the centuries, and of being forced to surrender their overseas markets to English merchants, were hardly less enthusiastic. Their parliament, more easily controlled than that in England, did give James an Act of Union, but unsupported by a reciprocal Act south of the border it was a dead letter. All that was salvaged from the plan was the repeal of some mutually hostile laws, an agreement by the English to return fugitives from Scottish justice, dual nationality for those born after the union of the crowns, and a reluctantly-flown union flag. Even this was withdrawn in 1634.

For most of the century England and Scotland remained separate and independent kingdoms. Each had its own parliament, laws, taxes and church. The problem for Scotland was that for much of the time her monarch was in voluntary exile south of the border. Within a single generation he came to regard himself as an Englishman who saw Scotland not as a separate nation but as just a northern province of his dominions. The mistake was disastrous.

THE HOUSE OF STUART 1603-1707/1807

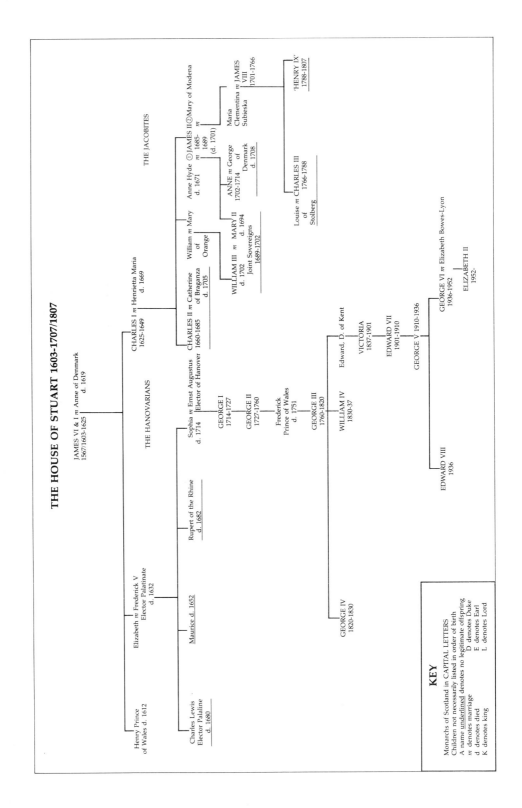

JAMES VI & I *m* Anne of Denmark
1567/1603-1625   d. 1619

Henry Prince
of Wales d. 1612

Elizabeth *m* Frederick V
Elector Palatinate
d. 1632

CHARLES I *m* Henrietta Maria
1625-1649   d. 1669

THE JACOBITES

THE HANOVARIANS

Charles Lewis
Elector Palatine
d. 1680

Maurice d. 1652

Rupert of the Rhine
d. 1682

Sophia *m* Ernst Augustus
d. 1714   Elector of Hanover

GEORGE I
1714-1727

GEORGE II
1727-1760

Frederick
Prince of Wales
d. 1751

GEORGE III
1760-1820

GEORGE IV
1820-1830

WILLIAM IV
1830-37

Edward, D. of Kent

VICTORIA
1837-1901

EDWARD VII
1901-1910

GEORGE V 1910-1936

EDWARD VIII
1936

GEORGE VI *m* Elizabeth Bowes-Lyon
1936-1952

ELIZABETH II
1952-

CHARLES II *m* Catherine
1660-1685   of Braganza
d. 1705

William *m* Mary
of
Orange

WILLIAM III *m* MARY II
d. 1702   d. 1694
Joint Sovereigns
1689-1702

Anne Hyde ① JAMES II ② Mary of Modena
d. 1671   *m*   1685-   *m*
1689
(d. 1701)

ANNE *m* George
1702-1714   of
Denmark
d. 1708

Louise *m* CHARLES III
of   1766-1788
Stolberg

Maria
Clementina *m* JAMES
Subieska   VIII
1701-1766

'HENRY IX'
1788-1807

KEY

Monarchs of Scotland in CAPITAL LETTERS
Children not necessarily listed in order of birth
A name underlined denotes no legitimate offspring
m denotes marriage   D denotes Duke
d denotes died   E denotes Earl
K denotes king   L denotes Lord

THE HOUSE OF STUART
1603 - 1707

The Stuarts were Scotland's foreign monarchs; they provided the country with some of its most incompetent and disliked rulers. The growing alienation of the Scots from their royal house and its administrators, which had bred national revolt and revolution, eventually led to full union between England and Scotland.

JAMES VI (continued)
JAMES I OF ENGLAND
1603 - 1625

During his time in England the fine reputation that James had acquired as King of Scotland was seriously undermined. But few kings have been more unjustly maligned. The carpings of xenophobic contemporaries about his physical appearance and personal behaviour have been accepted at their face value, while until recently his positive achievements have received scant recognition. The reasons for this are threefold. First, he had the misfortune to follow a popular and respected monarch whose reign, glorified by the singular naval successes of piratical freebooters (assisted by the weather) and dignified by a coincidental flowering of English letters, was to acquire a posthumous golden hue. Elizabeth's sex-appeal mysteriously translated itself down the centuries, ensnaring generations of frustrated middle-class male historians. At the time, however, many Englishmen viewed with a degree of relief the passing of an indecisive and parsimonious old queen, whose later years had been marked by high taxation, war and slump. Secondly, James was an outsider in a land of intolerant islanders. Although he did his best to master their sophisticated political system, he remained an alien whose errors and misunderstandings were magnified by his foreignness. Finally, James had the misfortune to be succeeded by a politically inept son. During the reign of Charles I (1625-49) the kingdoms of England and Scotland were beset by civil war. The search for long-term explanations of the governmental breakdown has cast an unduly critical light on the events of James' reign. Never have the sins of a son been more unkindly visited upon a father.

As King of England James found himself far nearer the centre of the European political stage than he had been in Scotland. He stepped from the wings to indulge in a magnificent diplomatic soliloquy, identifying himself as

'Rex Pacificus', the King of Peace, who would reconcile the warring Protestant and Catholic nations. To this end in 1613 he married off his daughter, Elizabeth, to the Protestant Prince Frederick V, Elector Palatine. He intended to balance this union with the marriage of one of his sons to a daughter of Spain's ruling house. When Henry Prince of Wales died of typhoid in 1612 his younger brother, Charles, was put forward in his place. The king's ambitious scheme, grand in conception but unrealistic in execution, was collapsing about him at the time of his death. Spain was never keen on the proposed marriage of one of her princesses to a heretic; ministers and ambassadors kept the idea alive just to prevent James becoming involved in the widespread European conflict which had broken out in 1618. When in 1623 Prince Charles and the royal favourite, George Villiers Duke of Buckingham, returned in humiliation from a supposedly secret viewing of what was on offer in Madrid, they joined the war party. By early 1625 open hostilities had broken out with Spain.

The Protestant link proved equally unfortunate. In 1618 Frederick rashly accepted the throne of Bohemia when the province rose up against the Habsburg Emperor of Austria. As the Habsburgs were also Spain's ruling family Spanish troops devastated Frederick's Palatinate, putting pressure on James to end his pacific policy and to join the general European fray. He wisely remained true to his principles, supporting his son-in-law only with a hopelessly inadequate expeditionary force under a German mercenary captain. However, James' grandiose scheme was in shreds. It had been unrealistic from the start. Nevertheless, perhaps it was understandable that a king raised in the relative poverty and international impotence of Scotland should overestimate the power and influence of the country he called Great Britain.

In most other respects James coped quite well in England. It took him a while to get the hang of the English parliament, where he had no Lords of the Articles committee to help him manage affairs. The squabbles of powerful rival court factions sometimes spilt over into parliament with unhappy results which raised issues of constitutional importance. Yet parliament was never united in opposition to the crown, even when bewildered by James' seemingly incessant demands for money. He lost none of his extravagance when he travelled south. The wealth of England enabled him to indulge in his expensive artistic tastes more lavishly than ever before, and there seemed no end to the largess sprinkled upon the favourites and fawners who hung about the court. The flattery and opulence did James no good either. They eased his insecurity, fed his vanity. Scarred with a number of unpleasant scandals, his court developed a seedy reputation. The government's debt mounted to an alarming £1m by the end of the reign. Above all, though, as far as Scots were concerned the sirens of the south had successfully seduced James away from home.

Before leaving for England in the spring of 1603 James delivered a farewell address at St Giles. The event was a moving one. As tears streamed down their faces, the king assured his audience of his love for them and promised to return to Scotland every three years. Perhaps, like fond parents bidding farewell to a son leaving home to make his way in the world, they wept because they realised that solemn undertakings made on such occasions are more easily made than kept. Events were to prove their apprehension well-founded. During the remaining 22 years of his life James returned to Scotland but once. Nevertheless, distant though the king might have been, Scotland continued to benefit from his intelligent if haphazard rule.

The theoretical head of state in James' absence was Louis Stewart, Duke of Lennox, the son of the king's teenage heart-throb, Esme Stewart (see Stewart family tree). In practice, power was being distilled more and more into the hands of the Privy Council. This group was further securing their influence — and thus that of the king — by sitting in the parliamentary committee known as the Lords of the Articles. This comprised eight men from each of the three parliamentary estates and eight royal nominees. By the end of James' reign it had become virtually a nominated assembly. They sat before parliament met, preparing forthcoming business which then frequently went through with a minimum of opposition. The leading members of the Privy Council were Lord President Thomas Hamilton ('Tam O' the Cowgate'), later created Earl of Melrose; the Earl of Dunbar, Treasurer to 1616, when he was replaced by the Earl of Mar; and Gideon Murray, Treasurer Depute 1612-21. Another key figure in the administration was John Spottiswoode, appointed Archbishop of Glasgow (1610), then of St Andrews (1615). The methods employed by James and his government in Scotland were not always scrupulous — more than once he ordered an adversary to the isolation of London where he could be dealt with as the king willed — but they were generally to the kingdom's advantage. Lawlessness declined, the economy flourished. With wealth came time and patronage for the arts; or, in the words of a more puritanical commentator, 'Peace begot Plenty and Plenty begot Ease and Wantonness'. Although towards the end of James' reign there were some signs that his authoritarian policies were resented, particularly as he was an absentee head of state, he showed enough political sense not to push matters too far. For his gifts of peace and plenty there was every reason for grateful Scots to name him 'Blessed King James'.

From London, James pursued Scottish lawbreakers with fewer scruples than he had shown when living among them. The Western Isles were one of his chief targets. To begin with he used the Earl of Argyll as his agent in the area, ably supported by Bishop Knox of the Isles. In 1608 a royal army under Andrew Stewart landed on Mull, the largest of the Inner Hebrides. Local clan chiefs were asked to gather on the island, invited to hear a sermon preached on a ship moored on the coast, then promptly kidnapped. Leaderless and confused, local clansmen on the surrounding islands were brought to justice. Revolts by the MacDonalds in 1614 and 1615 provoked equally fierce responses. The first was led by a man whose name and behaviour harked back to medieval times, Angus Og. He was hanged after his allies, the Campbells, had betrayed him to the royal forces. The next year the same punishment was

King James VI and I in an illumination from a Patent of Nobility. James' English subjects saw him as a foreigner and resented the hundreds of Scots who came south with him in 1603 in search of fortune and preferment. Despite this handicap, James generally coped well with the complex task of simultaneously governing his two kingdoms.

meted out to James' traitorous cousin Patrick Stewart, Earl of Orkney, and his son. Peace on the borders had been hastened by the Union of the Crowns and the few measures salvaged from the abortive attempt to integrate the two nations. Raiding subsided and nests of robbers were broken up. James hit upon an original device for ensuring that malefactors never again stirred up trouble, while at the same time putting their aggressive talents to good use: they were forcibly shipped off to Europe as soldiers in the armies employed in the endemic continental power struggles. They thus maintained — albeit unwillingly — a long-standing Scottish tradition of warrior export. For several years Sir William Cranston was empowered to patrol the borders with a special force of 25 mounted men-at-arms, a form of seventeenth-century flying squad. They were so successful that in 1621 they were considered no longer necessary and disbanded.

James believed that the kirk, in the form he left it in 1603, represented as unwarranted a threat to his personal authority as any lawbreaker. The King of England was undisputed Supreme Governor over a church which had not travelled as far down the road to Presbyterianism as that in Scotland. The Anglican church also permitted greater ceremony than James had been accustomed to; this too met with his approval. Therefore the king's aims for the church in Scotland were to make it more subject to his personal authority, and rather more flexible in its outlook. The two, obviously, were interlinked. The further a church moved from Rome, the more devolved its structure tended to be. No king who believed, as James did, that he had God-given responsibility to govern a state in its (and His) best interests could possibly look favourably upon a church with its own independent structure of presbyteries, synods and Assembly. The institution's hold on education and its nation-wide propaganda network gave it the power to make or break royal authority. (In an age without newspapers, radio or TV, and lacking a coherent system of local government responsible to the centre, the sermon was the surest way of passing information and moulding public opinion.) The key to the question, as James saw it, was the institution of bishops. James manipulated the kirk's General Assembly quite unscrupulously, outlawing in advance all those who attended its 1605 session. Of the 13 who dared to turn up, six were exiled for high treason. A Convention summoned the next year (later declared by the king to have been an Assembly!) established 'moderators' for each presbytery and district synod, positions ideally filled, at the higher level at least, by the bishops. Members of the episcopal bench were appointed by the king. In 1606 Melville and other possible objectors to the advancing royal authority were summoned to London. The Presbyterian leader was shut in the Tower for three years on a charge of mocking the English episcopacy. When he was released he was sent into exile, dying in Sedan 13 years later. In the meantime bishops had much of their landed wealth returned to them. By this means, in 1609 Scotland had in place a system of diocesan bishops which gave the king considerable control over the church. As in other fields of Scottish government, James' tactics had been less than honourable but he did not, for the time being at least, press his victory too far. The bishops he appointed were for the most part men of moderation and learning; in fact some of them were ex-Presbyterians. As long as Scots felt that the changes brought order rather than alteration in their religious life, the new arrangements were accepted. It was only when the king tried to take them a step further that he ran into serious opposition.

In 1616 a number of reforms of the church were planned which were to bring it more into line with English practice. These included a new liturgy as well as alterations in doctrine and ceremony. They were strongly resented. The following year James made his long overdue visit to Scotland, returning, he said, like a salmon to the place of its birth. He was determined to see his ecclesiastical changes implemented. But perhaps in his long absence he had forgotten the temperament of the subjects of his first kingdom. They would endure so much, but no more. The kirk had now been in place for over a generation and was firmly cemented in the hearts and minds of most Scots. They did not want it altered by a king who had, in their eyes, been perverted by English neo-popery. Parliament defeated the attempt to give the bishops greater authority. The new liturgy, containing much that had been lifted from the English Book of Common Prayer, was eventually dropped. All that the king managed to get through a bribed and browbeaten Assembly held at Perth in 1618 were the famous Five Articles. The first of these ordained that communion should be received in a kneeling position. To the Scots, who saw the ceremony as purely one of memorial, this smacked of the Catholic doctrine of Real Presence: the miraculous transformation of the substance of the bread and wine through the agency of a priest into the body and blood of Christ. Another article requested the observation of the major Christian festivals — undermining the kirk's teaching that the weekly Sabbath was the central holy day ordained by God. Confirmation by bishops further elevated the status of these left-overs from Roman Catholicism. Two further articles permitted private communion and baptism in cases where it seemed likely that the recipient was about to die. These two also appeared to resemble Catholic practices.

James had forced acceptance of this popish package on the unwilling Scots. But he had sufficient political sense, reinforced by his innate laziness and the difficulty of overseeing the church at a distance of 400 miles, not to demand their implementation with rigour. The innovations remained, in theory, part of the Scottish church's teaching and behaviour; in practice, guided by the wise moderation of Archbishop Spottiswoode, things went on much as they had done before.

King James VI was not an attractive man. He could sometimes be crude, even vulgar. A brittle arrogance half-hid a profound insecurity. His methods of dealing with adversaries could be devious and dishonourable. Despite all this, however, he served Scotland well, and to level at him the old epithet of 'the Wisest Fool in Christendom' is both to misunderstand his personality and belittle his achievements. One only has to compare the state of the nation in the year of his coronation, with how he left it in 1625 to realise that in King James VI, Scotland found one of her ablest monarchs.

CHARLES I
1625 - 1649

Born: 1600. Died: 1649. Marriage: Henrietta Maria. Children: Charles, James, Henry, Mary, Elizabeth, Anne, Katherine, Henrietta and a son (Charles) who died at birth.

Prince Charles was considered too unwell to accompany his father on the trimphant progress to England in the spring of 1603. Not until the next year was the sickly child considered fit enough to leave Scotland and join his family in their newly-acquired southern splendour. Largely isolated from the excesses of the Jacobean court, the boy then spent eight happy years, engaging in healthy country pursuits and acquiring a sound Renaissance education from his kindly Scots tutor, Thomas Murray. Charles learned to cope with the Classics as well as the more widely employed European languages such as French, Italian and Spanish; at the same time the seeds of an impeccable artistic taste were sown in his ordered, fastidious mind. He read quite widely, without the scholarly interest of his father. James' coarse manners were also alien to the boy who grew up aloof, reserved, correct and unimaginative. These characteristics were magnified when, after the death of his elder brother, Henry, in 1612, he found himself heir apparent to the thrones of Scotland and England. Although short in stature (a deficiency he sought to alleviate by wearing fashionable high-heeled shoes) he carried himself with dignity. His other natural handicap, a stammer, he was unable to mask: the fear of public humiliation which the impediment might bring increased his natural reserve.

Charles was burdened with a heavy sense of responsibility. Kingship was to him a sacred duty. Opposition to the crown was almost beyond his comprehension, and he viewed the church in both England and Scotland as a necessary support for monarchy. He was a devout man, too, attracted to ecclesiastical ceremony which accorded with his artistic preferences and supported his hierarchical view of society. For politics, with its compromises and petty deceits, he had no liking and had received little training. The results of this awkward blend of high church religion with political ineptitude were in the end to prove traumatic for Scotland and fatal for Charles. Not that he disliked or even disapproved of Scotland. Far from it — a contemporary observed that 'he was always an immoderate lover of the Scottish nation, having not only bene borne ther, but educated by that people and besiedged by

Stubborn and inflexible, Charles I was totally without the political skills necessary to govern seventeenth-century Britain. He was, however, a devoted family man and this relaxed portrait by van Honthurst captures something of the informal side of the king's personality which the public never saw.

them always'. Others noted that Charles' disjointed speech retained the trace of a Scots accent. But, Scotsman though he might have been by birth and blood, Charles was essentially English. His attachment to Scotland was largely romantic and dynastic, like that of innumerable second generation Scots exiles around the world who celebrate Burns night and Hogmanay with tears in their eyes, but who reject a trip 'home' as too expensive or incompatible with their expatriate employment. The Scots, on the other hand, retained a place in their hearts for the king they had loaned to England. They were so delighted in 1624 when his marriage to Henrietta Maria was announced — reawakening memories of the Auld Alliance — that the householders of Edinburgh were commanded to light a celebratory bonfire or risk a £20 fine. Harsh though their attacks on the royal prerogative were in the 1640s, very few Scots could stomach the execution of the king at the hands of Cromwell and his republican cronies. Charles II found widespread support when he landed in Scotland in June 1650.

Unlike most of the other Stewart monarchs, Charles was a devoted family man. His marriage to the sprightly 15-year-old French princess, Henrietta Maria, was troubled at first. She found him distant and reserved; he was irritated by her youthful gaity. However, they grew to love each other. The queen's Catholicism, which upset so many of their Scottish and English subjects, was tolerated by Charles, although he did not once contemplate conversion to Rome himself. During the difficult latter half of his reign he was always able to rely on the loyal support of his wife.

Fourteen years elapsed between James VI's departure from Scotland and his return in 1617. Charles left 29 years before he made the same costly journey, and then it was not so much as a pilgrim that he travelled north but as a missionary, bent on forceful conversion. He had been away too long.

During the king's absence the day-to-day government of Scotland was theoretically in the hands of his 47 Councillors, although with a quorum of only seven necessary for business most decisions were made by a handful of ministers, most important among whom was the Chancellor. Developments which did not augur well for the future were the steadily increasing number of bishops who found their way onto the Privy Council (nine by the mid-1630s) and the appointment of Archbishop Spottiswoode as Chancellor in 1635 — the first churchman to hold high secular office since the Reformation. In instigating such innovations Charles clearly did not know the stomach of his northern subjects. During the first six years of his reign his time was wholly taken up with the domestic and foreign problems which beset his government in England. This enabled his Scottish administration to flow along its accustomed channels with reasonable tranquility. As in the reign of James, men of relatively humble origin were employed as royal officers; commissions were set up to police the borders; and the bishop of the Isles and Privy Council kept a close eye on the Highlands, where local chiefs were engaged to keep their clansmen in order. Paternal concern for the people's welfare led to official encouragement for the establishment of parish schools.

The deceptive calm of these early years was shattered by Charles' religious policies. Other developments had been at work preparing the fertile soil in which revolt took root. Excluded from the positions of highest authority and influence, time hung uneasily on the hands of an under-employed nobility. There was no Versailles where they could at least pretend to exert influence. Expensively remote, the sophisticated English court appeared to welcome only flatterers or out-and-out episcopalians. Charles' 1625 Act of Revocation, although an expected measure at the start to a new reign, was disconcerting in both the underhand way it was presented and in the extent of its powers. After some compromise its effect was that all land that had once belonged to the church was now held for the crown, in return for payments to support the clergy. The estates of many nobles were affected. Their sense of unease mounted for the king now had the theoretical right to deprive them at a stroke of all the land they held from him. Other factors raised the political temperature: the continued high-handed control of parliament by the Lords of the Articles (the 1634 parliament rubber stamped 168 Acts in a single day!); a measure taking back all hereditable offices into the hands of the crown; the maintenance of a direct taxation system (which in practice had become annual by the 1630s); exploitation of the royal right to grant monopolies; and the inordinately high financial demands made on Edinburgh, now officially recognised as the capital city of the kingdom.

James I had been attracted by the ceremony, theology and royal authority of the Church of England. He would have liked to bring the Scottish church much more into line with its southern counterpart but had the political sense not to press his demands too far. From the beautiful remote calm of Whitehall his elegant son also viewed the ecclesiastical arrangements of his other kingdom with distaste. Since ascending the throne he had come increasingly under the influence of an earnest high-church cleric by the name of William Laud, a man against whom Charles had been warned by his perspicacious father. The king and his archbishop (Laud was appointed to Canterbury in 1633) wanted an ordered and disciplined episcopalian church in both England and Scotland, firmly under royal control, and in which God could be worshipped in 'the beauty of holiness'. To many subjects in both kingdoms much that they did smacked of popery. The Scots were given their first glimpse of the new order in 1633 at Charles' belated coronation, performed with sumptuous Anglican ceremony in Holyrood palace. From the singing of the choirs and the grandeur of splendid bishops around the little arrogant king, to the liturgy uttered in strange English accents (indistinguishable from Latin to some untutored Scots ears), to a Presbyterian the service might as well have been Roman Catholic. Worse was to follow.

Unsupported by the vote of either parliament or a General Assembly, Charles used an assumed royal supremacy to order a new code of canons and liturgy for his Scottish church. Mutterings of discontent grew to rumblings of revolt. When the revised liturgy was introduced in July 1637, rebellion finally erupted. It started with a riot in St Giles Cathedral in Edinburgh and spread rapidly over the whole of the southern part of the country. Royal proclamations were ignored. In December, representatives from the church, nobility, towns and lairds set up a rebel steering committee known as 'the Tables'. James Leslie, Earl of Rothes, and James Graham, Earl of Montrose, emerged as leaders of the nationalist movement. The following February the celebrated National Covenant was drawn up, skillfully constructed by the talented minister Alexander Henderson and the lawyer Archibald Johnston. It began with the 'Negative Confession' which James VI had accepted in 1581, then listed all parliamentary Acts incompatible with the recent royal innovations. It ended with rousing but unspecific statements about people's rights and liberties, the importance of parliament, and the need for people to pledge themselves to defend the king and their true religion. The Covenant oath was sworn in the churchyard of Greyfriars church, Edinburgh, first by the nobility (Montrose's name heading all others), then by ministers and their congregations. Copies were swiftly carried all over the country; thousands added their signatures.

King Charles had a full-scale national revolt on his hands. Such was the extraordinary extent of his isolation, however, that he believed that this 'small cloud in the North' would soon blow over. He dithered, ordering his commissioner and cousin, the Marquis of Hamilton, to use what tactics he would to hold the Scots 'until I be ready to suppress them'. Concessions were made; but they were too few and too late. The boulder of rebellion rolled inexorably towards war. In November 1638 the General Assembly of the church met — for the first time in 20 years — and proceeded, quite illegally, to dismantle the church established by parliament in the reigns of James VI and his son. Moderate episcopalians took fright at the increasingly radical turn of events and for the first time the opposition to the king began to divide. Charles unfortunately lacked the skill to turn this to his advantage. Faced by experienced Scottish veteran soldiers, many of whom had returned home from fighting with the great continental Protestant generals, the king's hastily gathered forces sensibly chose not to fight. In June 1639 a temporary peace was made at Berwick, Charles promising to summon a Scottish parliament and legal Assembly. If he had been strongly supported by his English subjects, Charles might have been able to make more of a stand against the Scots. As it was, his tactlessness and political incompetence had already alienated him from the English almost as effectively as from the Scots.

In England the first years of Charles' reign had gone badly. His attachment to his father's favourite, George Villiers (created Duke of Buckingham in 1623) separated the king from the political nation until the Duke's assassination in 1628. War with both France and Spain put the constitution under dangerous strain as the government was forced to resort to highly unpopular methods of raising funds. At the same time the religious policy which later drove the Scots into rebellion added to the administration's

James Graham, 1st Marquis of Montrose (1612-50) at first joined the Covenanters in their campaign against Charles I's religious innovations, but he was alarmed at the extremism which followed and during the English Civil War fought a brilliant campaign for the king. Montrose was executed in May 1650 after the failure of an attempt to restore Charles II. This highly-charged picture by J. Drummond is an attempt to convey the romantic appeal of Montrose's daring military exploits.

unpopularity. Exacerbated by bitter factional squabbles, unease at the direction the government was taking manifested itself in a number of parliamentary measures which were to assume major significance in the light of the constitutional upheavals later in the reign. In 1629 Charles dismissed parliament and decided to rule as best he could without it. His 'Personal Rule' was marked by heavy-handed paternalism in both England and Ireland, an increasingly mistrusted religious policy, and unprecedented attempts to raise money by use of the royal prerogative. The upshot of all this was that when the king called upon the English to rally round him against the Scots they refused to do so. It is a measure of Charles' supreme ineptitude that he succeeded in uniting against him the subjects of two nations who until recently had regarded each other with undisguised scorn.

At Berwick Charles had agreed to summon the estates (parliament) and an Assembly of the church. The latter met first, without bishops, and proceeded to ratify the proceedings of the previous year's unofficial Assembly. It then demanded that the new royal commissioner, Traquair, and the council make the Covenant obligatory on all Scots. Parliament endorsed this and introduced a whole string of measures which amounted to a revolution. A Triennial Act ensured that parliament would meet every three years, whether called by the king or not. The clerical estate was abolished. All royal officers had to be appointed in consultation with parliament. Scotland had in effect become a theocracy. Real power lay with parliament's Committee of the Three Estates and the Assembly's Commission. The leading figure was Archibald Campbell, Earl of Argyll. Presbyterian rule, under which church attendance was compulsory and dissenters persecuted, was as intolerant as the regime which the revolution had displaced. Meanwhile, there had been several significant developments elsewhere.

In August 1640 Montrose and 17 nobles formed the Cumbernauld Bond to protect what they saw as the Convenant's true aims against political extremism and private gain. They were displeased with Argyll's exploitation of the situation for his own ends. In the conservative northern parts of the kingdom and in the universities of St Andrews and Glasgow there was similar hostility to the new regime. But the Covenanters, commanded by the outstanding general Alexander Leslie (whom Charles created Earl of Leven in 1641), still possessed the military strength to cow their opponents. In contact with English parliamentary leaders, Leslie had invaded northern England in the late summer of 1640, brushed aside Charles' forces and occupied Newcastle. At Ripon the Scots agreed to advance no further, in return for a maintenance payment of £850 a day. The king visited Scotland a year later to agree the Covenanters' stringent peace terms. In November he returned south, leaving the question of church reform open. Moreover, he had done his cause no good by scheming to win opposition leaders to his side and plotting to kidnap some of them. A year later civil war had broken out in England. Urgent requests for assistance from Charles and his opponents led to widespread debate north of the border as to which side, if any, they should support.

The Privy Council urged the nation to back their king. The standing committee of the Assembly (calling themselves Conservators of the Peace) favoured the Roundheads, who were prepared to profess a cynical liking for the Presbyterian system. Leading Covenanters believed Scottish participation in the English war would be akin to a crusade. The Solemn League and Covenant was the document which seduced the Scots from their king. It offered the prospect of a single Presbyterian church stretching from the Orkneys to the Isle of Wight, and even west to Ireland. An Assembly of Divines meeting at Westminster drew up a Directory of Public Worship, Confession of Faith, catechisms and a book of metrical Psalms. Although the Assembly was staffed by Englishmen, with Scots attending only in an advisory capacity, its creations were eventually implemented only north of the border.

The war brought out a new side in Charles' character. He showed himself to be a brave and skillful general. However, his political failings had made his position more precarious than it used to be. For a while a brilliant campaign by the Earl of Montrose, who had finally parted with Argyll and the Covenanters in 1644, looked as if it might win all Scotland for the Royalists. Defeat at Philiphaugh on 12th September 1645 terminated his outstanding run of victories. The Covenanters took bloody revenge, slaughtering the women and children who followed Montrose's army, and going on to further attrocities, such as hanging 36 of the Earl's Lamont supporters from a single tree. Fear of Montrose's Highlanders had made Leslie unwilling to march deep into England. Nevertheless his experienced soldiers played a crucial part in the defeat of Prince Rupert's army at Marston Moor (2nd July 1644), after which he ensured that the north of England remained in the hands of the king's enemies. By late 1645 the English parliament's New Model Army had overcome Charles' forces in the south. With parliamentary troops tightening the net around his Oxford headquarters, Charles decided to flee. With his beautiful long hair cropped short with a knife and his elegant beard similarly disfigured, he made his way through the enemy lines disguised as a servant named Harry. At first he seemed unsure which way to go. Should he make for the continent, rally his support there and try to win back his kingdoms with an invasion? Or should he continue his struggle by diplomacy, seeking to divide his ill-assorted enemies? The king made up his mind as he rode. Changing his disguise, he turned north. A few days later, to the considerable surprise of all parties, he presented himself at Leslie's camp outside Newark. He had always professed to love the Scots nation. Now that love was put to the test.

In the dangerous political game that was being played between the king, the English parliament, the growing band of English independents (those who wanted no state church at all), and the Covenanters, the latter now held the trump card. How and when were they to play it? In fact the Scots did not know what to do. The two things they wanted were incompatible: king and Covenant. 'This damned covenant', Charles wrote to his queen in France, 'is the product of Rebellion and breeds nothing but treason'. After fruitless negotiation the Covenanters simply marched out of Newcastle, where they had been based, leaving Charles behind to see how the English would manage him. The fact that at the time of their departure the Scots were paid some of the money they were owed by the English parliament gave rise to the accusation from the king that he had been sold. The charge was hardly fair. Before long many of those against whom Charles was railing had laid down their lives on his behalf.

The last act of Charles' strange eventful reign began at Christmas 1647. After the departure of the Scots the king was a prisoner of the English parliament, among whom were quite a few Presbyterians. By the summer of 1647 the New Model Army had become an important political force as well as an unstoppable military machine. The lower ranks were attracted to the beliefs of the Levellers, the officers (or 'grandees') spoke of less radical but nevertheless significant political reform. Both groups were united in mistrust of the king and a dislike of Presbyterianism. In a well-executed raid that summer they seized the king. Like Baron Frankenstein, the English parliament discovered that they had created a child whom they could no longer control. Charles' devious mind was continually hatching schemes for both his physical and political escape. In November he got away as far as the Isle of Wight where, on 27th December, he signed the Engagement with a number of leading Scots. By its terms, which undermined the Solemn League and Covenant, England was to try Presbyterianism for three years, the army was to be disbanded and extremist sects put down. The Scots were to provide military help to see the arrangement implemented, and Royalist risings were planned in different parts of England.

In Scotland there had been a widespread reaction against the extremism of the Presbyterian Assembly and the indignities forced upon the captive king. The Engagement was the result of this reaction. Nevertheless, as the agreement was unacceptable to the Assembly, it was a divided nation which sent its army south in support of the king. In the so-called Second Civil War the Scots and the Royalists failed to co-ordinate their efforts. Galvanised into unity by the threat to its supremacy, the New Model Army crushed the English revolts and destroyed the Scottish army in a series of battles fought near Preston between 17th and 19th August. The position of King Charles was now very dangerous. The dominant power in both kingdoms was the English army, which had finally dispensed with the polite fiction that they were fighting for a king led astray by wicked advisors, and openly condemned him as 'a man of blood'. In their eyes he was no longer a sovereign monarch, but merely Charles Stuart. In Scotland the Engagers had been scattered by a rising from the south-west known as the 'Whiggamore Raid'. The fervent Presbyterians were in charge once more. United by a common antipathy towards Charles, the theocrats welcomed Cromwell's troops into Edinburgh. Cromwell was now coming to be seen as the pivotal power in the land. When he left Scotland to deal with the king, he left behind a strong garrison of English troops under the command of

Charles II once declared himself 'an ugly fellow' and his looks certainly did not improve with age, as this portrait attributed to Thomas Hawker rather candidly illustrates. Although lazy, Charles was drawn towards absolutism and his absentee governance of Scotland allowed for participation by scarcely more than a handful of the political nation.

Major-General Lambert.

The last scene took place on 30th January 1649. Despite sincere but impotent Scottish protests, Cromwell's army had established a court of dubious legality, tried the king and condemned him to death. To the end Charles carried himself with much dignity. At his trial his stammer left him and he spoke with clarity and sense, denying the authority of the court. When the sentence was passed — 'the said Charles Stuart, as a tyrant, traitor, murtherer, and a public enemy, shall be put to death, by the severing of his head from his body' — he was jostled from the hall before he could make formal reply. 'I am not suffered for to speak,' he warned, 'expect what justice other people will have.' On the day of execution he repeated his view that 'a subject and sovereign are clean different things', and that by executing their king the people were destroying the very foundations of their own land and liberty. 'I am the Martyr of the people', he proclaimed. Lest he struggle and the huge crowd become agitated, he was afforded a smaller block than was customary, forcing him to face execution lying almost flat. His head was removed with a single blow. The 17-year-old Philip Henry was one of those who had gathered to witness the gruesome event. He later recorded in his diary:

> The blow I saw given, and can truly say with a sad heart, the instant whereof, I remember well, there was such a groan by the thousands then present as I never heard before and desire I may never hear again.

The groan was mighty indeed, for it carried the length of the kingdom to the ears of astounded Scots. As far as they were concerned the English could do what they wished with their own king. But Charles was not just king of England; he was king of Scotland too. The English had no right whatsoever to murder their monarch without so much as consulting them.

CHARLES II
1649 - 1685

Born: 1630. Died: 1685. Marriage: Catherine of Braganza. No children.

It was fitting that the first child of Charles I and Henrietta Maria to survive the rigours of seventeenth-century childbirth should have been the fruit of the couple's growing love for one another. The future Charles II was the first Scottish monarch since the 'Maid of Norway' to be born outside Scotland, a country for which he never professed any great affection. The rift between the Scots and their monarchs, begun when James VI emigrated in 1603 and widened during the civil wars of his son's reign, assumed the proportions of a canyon under the third Stuart. It is significant that despite all the turmoil when Charles I was on the throne it was only during his son's time that a few influential Scots first began to question the need for a monarchy at all. The Union of the Crowns worked without fuller political union as long as the Scots retained some emotional bond with the king who was directing their affairs. Charles II's failure to visit Scotland after 1660, coupled with his high-handed long-range government and an unsatisfactory choice of ministers, meant that as far as Scotland was concerned the system established by his grandfather became increasingly unsatisfactory.

The first 10 years of Charles' life were happy enough. Although his mother expressed disappointment, even alarm, at the child's swarthy complexion, she was proud of him and Charles I was a preoccupied but affectionate father. The boy's education does not seem to have been unduly strict or academically exacting. He had a quick mind and picked up without too much difficulty the classical, artistic and utilitarian subjects placed before him. However he was not bookish and as with most boys of his age, his chief interests lay in the outdoor pursuits. William Cavendish, Earl of Newcastle, the prince's only Gentleman of the Bedchamber, was a major influence on the way he was brought up, encouraging him in practical rather than theoretical studies. At the age of eight Charles had his own household and held his own court at Richmond. About Scotland he seems to have been told little and cared even less. He was by birth and upbringing an Englishman.

The Covenant and Bishops' Wars made little difference to the prince's lifestyle. Their repercussions on England, however, catapulted him into the adult world of politics and war. Charles and his younger brother James were present at the first battle of the Civil War, fought at Edgehill in the autumn of 1642. The 12-year-old boy does not appear to have been frightened by the noise and butchery of battle; at one stage in the fighting he had to be restrained lest he charge headlong into the mêlée himself. Nevertheless, the war was over before Charles was able to play a significant part in it. He saw his father for the last time on 4th March 1645. Exactly a year later he landed on the Scilly Isles, an impecunious refugee from the kingdoms he had been born to govern.

From the Scilly Isles Charles sailed to Jersey, then joined his mother in Paris. Here, as so many adolescant visitors to the city before and after him, he was introduced to the pleasures of the flesh which were to remain his favourite spare-time activity. He may also have developed a penchant for French women: among the several mistresses who graced his court in later years pride of place was held by Louise de Kerouaille, whom Charles met in 1670.

In 1648 Charles moved to Calais then to Holland, from where he made an attack on the Thames as his contribution to the Second Civil War. He then contracted a mild but dangerous attack of smallpox. There is a story that at the time of his father's trial Charles sent a sheet of paper to the English parliament, blank apart from his signature at the bottom. MPs were invited to write on it whatever terms they wished for preserving the king's life. The failure of this device and other pleas for clemency was made apparent to the prince when, in the first week of February 1649, he was greeted by one of his chaplains with the auspicioius title 'Your Majesty'.

The response of the Scots to news of the execution of Charles I was straightforward. At the cross in Edinburgh Lord Chancellor Loudon read a proclamation, 'K. Charles behedit at Whytehall gate, in England … one Tuesday, the 30 of Januarij, 1649 … Prince Charles [is] proclaimed King of Grae Britane, France and Irland …'. England was a republic and, whether he liked it or not, Charles had to devote his attention to the kingdoms which still accepted him. For a while he delayed. He hoped that the Irish, who had also announced his accession, might present him with a launching pad for an assault on England. He also backed a military expedition to northern Scotland by that most skillful of royalist commanders, the Marquis of Montrose. Charles was fearful of the price the Covenanters might demand for their support. As it turned out, the Irish were overwhelmed by Cromwell, and Montrose was defeated at Carbisdale. Never a man of much principle, Charles disowned his erstwhile general and landed in Scotland on 23rd June 1650. Montrose had been hanged and dismembered in Edinburgh the previous month. The events of the next year were both disappointing and humiliating for Charles and may well have played a part in framing his future policies towards the northern kingdom. No doubt sheltering behind massive mental reservations, he signed the Covenants of 1638 and 1643, and agreed to condemn his father's faults and mother's idolatory. Although he was treated with respect, Charles was irked by the sermonising of the Presbyterians and their supervision of his private life. Ironically, it was Oliver Cromwell who temporarily set him free.

Fresh from his victories in Ireland, Cromwell moved north in July 1650. In theory England and Scotland were still bound to each other, but Charles' alliance with Catholic Irish and the insistence of the Covenanters that they were supporting the monarch of both kingdoms was in Cromwell's mind sufficient justification for his action. Skilled though the Scots' defence was, at Dunbar on 3rd September they allowed Cromwell to fight a battle on his own terms. The Covenanting army was destroyed. Charles must have received the news of Dunbar with mixed feelings. Extreme Covenanters (known as the 'Remonstrants') rejected him, thereby freeing him to form an alliance with the royalists and moderate Presbyterians in a group (led by Argyll and the Committee of the Three Estates) known as the 'Resolutioners'. The 'Holy Army' of the Remonstrants was defeated by Major-General Lambert. Charles was crowned at Scone on New Year's Day 1651, receiving the crown from Argyll. He was the last king to partake of such a ceremony with the ancient Scottish Regalia.

When the New Model Army took Edinburgh castle and moved on Perth from the east, Charles slipped by them to the west and began a daring march into England known as 'the Start'. To Charles' intense disappointment few joined the ranks of his well-ordered army as it moved rapidly south. The new regime in England might not be liked, but its military prowess was respected and feared. At Worcester on 3rd September, the anniversary of Dunbar, Charles discovered why: Cromwell cut the royalist army to pieces. The story of Charles' subsequent escape is well-known. With the aid of loyal subjects, many of whom were Catholic, he used disguises, priest holes and even an oak tree to evade capture, eventually making his way once more to France and his mother's court. It was almost nine years before he returned to England. He never saw Scotland again.

Charles' second exile was longer and more miserable than his first. Brought up lacking little that money could buy and expecting to inherit one of Europe's more presigious monarchies, he found himself rejected by his subjects (or at least by that group of them who wielded power). He was embarrassingly short of funds and treated as scarcely more than a pawn in other nations' diplomatic exchanges. It is little wonder that when he returned to Britain he resolved 'never to go on his travels again'. Relations with his mother became strained. The only force nominally under his control was a number of ships, but they had been whisked off to the West Indies by Prince Rupert who, having ultimately failed as a commander of land forces, was now trying his hand at piracy. Nevertheless, Charles did what he could to find a way back to the thrones from which he was excluded. He was in close touch with the Highlanders who rose unsuccessfully on his behalf in 1654 and at one time planned to join them in person. The next year he stood behind the royalist rising in England, but it also collapsed in ignominious failure. In 1656, based at Louvain in the Spanish Netherlands, he struck up an agreement with the Spanish who had recently commenced hostilities with the Cromwellian regime. He even assembled a little invasion force of his own, which he hoped to ship over to Britain with Spanish assistance. In the end, however, it was not so much his actions as those of his divided countrymen after the death of Oliver Cromwell which enabled him to return in triumph in 1660. The most positive gesture that Charles made towards this happy conclusion to his exile was ensuring, particularly in the skillfully worded Declaration of Breda, that he offered all things to all men. All Englishmen, that is. Like the execution of his father, the restoration of Charles II was imposed on Scotland without consultation.

The years between the Battle of Worcester and the return of Charles II were the only time in Scottish history when the entire country was conquered and held in subjection for any length of time by a foreign power. Neither the Romans, nor the Normans, nor the Plantaganets had been able to impose their will on Scotland as Cromwell was to do. Yet the experience was not altogether an unhappy one. When the Cromwellian union came to an end not a few Scots were sorry at its passing, for it had brought efficient, tolerant government.

The conquest of Scotland was all but completed with the capture of

Dunnottar castle early in 1652. A few Highlanders, such as Sir Ewan Campbell (who did not surrender before he had bitten out the throat of an English officer trying to arrest him), clung on for a while longer. But the well-disciplined troops of General Monck were ultimately irresistible. An army of between 10,000 and 18,000 men dominated the country, operating from the four large forts which they threw up at strategic points. They ensured that the administration — which included Scotsmen — was obeyed, and law and order was well maintained. The church functioned much as before, although without bishops or an Assembly, and without the right to persecute those who did not see eye to eye with its theology. There were some wise reforms, such as the substitution of English for Latin in the courts, and after the considerable disruption and hardship of years of war there were signs of returning prosperity. Union with England was effected practically in 1652, although it was not given sanction by parliament until 1657. The Scots were granted 30 MPs at Westminster, a miserable representation. Not surprisingly they were seen by an English MP as 'like a wooden leg tied to a natural body'.

Forward-looking and reasonable though the administration of the English was, the people of Scotland could not help feeling that their experience had been 'as when the poor bird is embodied into the hawk that hath eaten it up'. They greeted the restoration of Charles II with wild rejoicing. Edinburgh in particular caught on to the festival atmosphere, marking the event with cannon fire, drums, trumpets and fireworks, and even paid for a drinking fountain to run with claret. The country was celebrating its renewed independence and, it hoped, a reduction in the considerable burden of taxation demanded by the upkeep of the English army. Yet if the Scots had known how the reign of Charles II was to turn out, they might not have capered with such glee. Backed by an oath compulsory on all office holders in church and state, proclaiming the king the 'only Supreme Governor of this Kingdom, over all persons and in all causes', Charles controlled Scotland from London with near-total authority. 'Never', commented a percipient sympathiser, 'was a king so absolute as in poor old Scotland'.

The king's absolutist style probably came more from a desire to avoid the sort of troubles which had recently torn his kingdoms apart than a conscious quest for power for its own sake. He believed that consultative government could all too easily lead to contested government. Above all he wished for a quiet and peaceful life, unruffled by faction, strife or bigotry, in which he could indulge in his straightforward pleasures without disturbance and his subjects could go unhindered about their business. His experience, in France as well as Scotland and England, had led him to believe that the only way this could come about was through the offices of an hereditary monarch of unchallenged authority. His role model was his cousin, Louis XIV of France. Experience had also taught Charles that, whatever one's ultimate goals, survival came first. Unlike his father or his brother, Charles would never lose his kingdoms on a matter of principle. He was a pragmatist, a politician. If the truth was compromising, he would lie. At times of crisis, if he felt that direct and positive action might not succeed, he would do nothing but agree with the majority and bide his time. This clever, cold man showed greater concern for his dogs and mistresses than for those who joined in the political game. When the circumstances demanded, he disowned his mother and father; having urged Montrose into rebellion on his behalf, he rejected him when he failed; Argyll, the man who had crowned him in 1651, he had executed 10 years later; at the height of England's Exclusion Crisis (1679-81) he even considered turning against his brother in order to save his own position. Yet when he died the authority of the crown in both England and Scotland was greater than it had been for over a century.

The popular image of Charles is very different. Superficially at least he gave the impression of being anything but tyrannical. His popular nickname is the 'Merry Monarch', remembered more for his frolics with the likes of Nell Gwynn than for unscrupulous duplicity. The nation could identify with his petty sins and — most important in any monarch — he had the common touch. He was as comfortable jesting with country people during one of his progresses through England as he was with presiding over the court in London. He was an inveterate (and repetitive) story-teller with a sharp sense of humour and a good memory. His approach to life was what we might now term laid-back, but which has more commonly been called lazy. All who met him were struck by his charm. Not that Charles was much to look at. 'Odd's fish,' he once announced disconcertingly, 'I am an ugly fellow!' He was over six foot tall with a dark skin that during his exile earned him the name 'Black Boy'. His large, fleshy face, which as he grew older looked increasingly as if it had been fashioned out of brown dough, featured a large broad nose and bright black eyes beneath heavy brows. His wife was the dull but patient Catholic Portuguese princess, Catherine of Braganza. She had little influence on policy, although her religion made her the centre of anti-Catholic rumour. She failed to provide Charles with any children owing to a condition which may well have been known before their marriage. Charles treated her with respect and kindness, if not with fidelity. As one might expect from a man who signed the Covenants yet may have died a shrived Roman Catholic, his religious faith was lightly held; whatever he might have believed in his heart, he did not allow his personal faith to stand in the way of practical politics.

Although history's timepiece can move only one way, the Restoration saw a concerted effort to put back the clock to pre-Covenanting times. Restored were the king, parliament, privy council and judicature. The moderate episcopal church of Charles' grandfather was also re-established, and the king was wise enough to see that apart from seats on the council for the two archbishops, clerics did not hold important positions in secular government. Many of the traditional nobility and gentry — the class whose alienation had enabled the revolution of 1637-41 to take place — returned to privilege and at least local influence. Covenants and conventicles (unofficial prayer meetings) were banned in a vast sweep of parliamentary legislation, the more dramatic feature of which was the Act Recissory (1662) which repealed all Acts passed since 1633. Although Charles had little time for Presbyterianism, regarding it as 'not a religion for gentlemen', presbyteries and synods were reinstated, but the General Assembly was not. In 1664 the church was given a Court of High Commission. About 270 ministers (perhaps a quarter of the total) were deprived of their livings for refusing to accept episcopal collation. Parliament, which voted the king £480,000 a year for life, was not regularly summoned but was freer to oppose the government than had sometimes been the case in the past. By and large, Charles' restoration settlement, involving only four executions, was quite realistic and broadly-based. The majority of Scots — not that they had much choice in the matter — accepted it without complaint. The exceptions were the strict Covenanters, for whom their original oath was perpetual and indissoluble. Unlike Charles, compromise was not in their nature.

The king kept a close personal eye on Scottish affairs. His representative north of the border was his commissioner, whose symbolic touching of an Act of Parliament signified the royal assent. Effective power remained in London where the key figure, apart from the king, was the Secretary of State for Scotland, responsible for passing on to the king and council all letters and messages from Scotland and conveying the government's wishes in the other direction. From 1661 until he had a stroke in 1680 the post was filled by John Maitland, Earl and then Duke of Lauderdale. In 1669 he increased his power by becoming commissioner as well. Lauderdale, one of the original covenanters, a framer of the Solemn League and Covenant and representative at the Westminster Assembly of Divines, had returned to the royalist cause by joining the Engagers who fought for Charles I in the Second Civil War. After the Battle of Worcester (1651) he was held in the Tower of London until released at the Restoration. With the fall of Commissioner Middleton in 1663 Lauderdale was second only to the king in Scotland, a position used by the Duke and his family to accumulate a considerable fortune. (It is said that as commissioner alone he made £18,000 a year.) Corruption and injustice were rife.

Since the Union of the Crowns, Scotland's foreign policy had been forced to follow in the wake of England's. When an Anglo-Dutch war broke out in 1665 there was some sympathy for the Presbyterian enemy. This helped provoke the Covenanters' Pentland Rising in the south-west. The rebels found little sympathy in the rest of the country and were mercilessly put down, despite the king's advocation of clemency. There then followed a period of conciliation to 1673. The army was reduced, and two Declarations of Indulgence relaxed the laws against conventicles and made life easier for Presbyterian ministers. Although this divided the nonconformists, drawing the more moderate ones to the government, it also enabled the enthusiasts to expand their proselytising, and so led to a second wave of prosecution. Death was instituted as the penalty for preaching at a conventicle. In 1678 the government's campaign reached new heights of ferocity when troops of the

'Highland Host' (actually including many Lowlanders) were quartered on disaffected Covenanters. Cruelty was met with cruelty: the next year Archbishop Sharp of St Andrews, a confirmed episcopalian and arch enemy of the extremists, was savagely murdered. He had been travelling home with his daughter in an unescorted coach when he was spotted by some Covenanting desperadoes. Having failed in an attempt to shoot him, they dragged him from his coach and hacked him to death.

Sharp's murder sparked off a small-scale civil war. The armed Covenanters of the south-west coalesced around the Rutherglen Declaration and at Drumclog in Lanarkshire defeated government troops under John Graham of Claverhouse. They then proceeded to Glasgow where they started to wrangle among themselves. Charles sent north his favourite illegitimate son, John Scott, Duke of Monmouth, who scattered the rebels at Bothwell Brig. Influenced by the king and Monmouth, government policy towards the rebels was at first clement. An Act of Indemnity was passed and Charles issued a further Declaration of Indulgence.

In 1680 a new figure took charge of Scottish affairs: the king's fervently Roman Catholic brother James, Duke of Albany and York. Repression was resumed. Lead by Richard Cameron a tiny group of fanatics, known as the Cameronians, kept up the struggle. They disowned the king, preferring 'King Jesus'. Despite defeat at Airds Moss they maintained their efforts through guerilla tactics for the remainder of Charles' reign and throughout that of his brother. Ghastly attrocities were committed on both sides, blackening the reputations of the royalist commanders Claverhouse ('Bluidy Clavers') and Sir George Mackenzie ('Bluidy Mackenzie'). This tragic period of Scottish history has come to be known as the 'Killing Time'.

Having smoothed the way for the accession of a Catholic monarch, James retired south again in 1682, leaving a reputation that did not augur well for the future. Charles lived on to 1685. His life, as the Scottish bishop Burnet recalled, 'was one of the greatest instances in history of the various revolutions that ever could befall any one man'. He had not cared much for Scotland but he had presided over several years of relative peace and increasing prosperity, during which the country witnessed advances in areas such as science, literature and architecture. Above all, however, the lesson of the reigns of Charles II and his father was that the person of the monarch was no longer essential for the maintenance of the Scottish nation. Originally the figure of the king or queen had acted as a magnet, holding together the various pieces of the kingdom when they threatened to fly off. Now the nation of Scots had coalesced with secure administration and culture. The time was fast approaching when it would no longer be necessary to maintain the fiction of an independent Scottish monarchy in London.

JAMES VII
1685 - 1689 (James II of England)

Born: 1633. Died: 1701. Marriage: (1) Anne Hyde; (2) Mary of Modena. Children: By Anne Hyde: Charles, James, Charles, Edgar, Henrietta and Catherine; By Mary of Modena: Charles, James, Catherine, Charlotte and Louisa.

James VII was 52 when he inherited the Scottish throne from his brother Charles II. Superfically the two men were quite alike. They both had large lugubrious faces set with heavy eyebrows and fleshy lips. James was a fairly tall, physically vigorous man, who shared his brother's almost insatiable desire for women. Yet the contrasts between the brothers were far more striking than any similarities. Where Charles was dark, James was fair-haired and light-skinned. Where Charles was easy-going, unprincipled and amoral, James was sincere, earnest and fervent in his political and religious beliefs. This made him a poor politician and prone to waves of guilt at his sexual behaviour. His whole manner lacked flexibility. Charles' mournful expression would light up when something happened to interest or amuse him, while James' retained a permanent air of melancholy. As a young man James was brave and dashing, though he tended to rush into ventures without fully thinking them through. He wrote well, despite an indifferent formal education but he did not have the sharp insights of Charles; while the elder brother was still on the throne a contemporary wrote: 'The King could see things if he would; the Duke would see things if he could.'

James made two marriages. The first was to Anne Hyde, the daughter of his brother's chief minister, the Earl of Clarendon. She was James' mistress while they were still in exile on the continent and when she became pregnant in 1659 he made a secret promise to marry her. He kept his word and made her his wife the next year, despite bitter complaints that a woman of her relatively lowly birth was no fit bride for the heir apparent. This hostility mounted when Anne converted to Roman Catholicism and was accused of urging her husband to follow suit. She died in 1671. Two years later James married the attractive 14-year-old Mary of Modena. She was a lively child who grew to tolerate James' plodding infidelities with a maturity born of inevitability. By his first wife James had six children, all but two of whom died young. The surviving daughters, Mary and Anne, were both to rule as queens in their own right. James had five more children by his second wife: a son and heir christened James (born 1688), a delightful daughter, Louisa Maria Theresa, and three others who did not see adulthood. Any list of James' offspring should probably include the four children he had by his mistress Arabella Churchill, the sister of John Churchill, future Duke of Marlborough and direct ancestor of Winston Churchill, Britain's celebrated wartime leader.

Shortly after his birth James was created Duke of York, the traditional title of an English monarch's second son. In 1660 he acquired the equivalent Scottish title, Duke of Albany. The prince's education was seriously disrupted by the outbreak of civil war in 1642. He joined his brother as a spectator at the Battle of Edgehill in October and was then taken to the royalist headquarters at Oxford, where he stayed for the remainder of the war. For some extraordinary reason the young prince had a penchant for dwarves in these early years and his household was rarely without one. After the king's defeat he was detained by parliament and deprived of his diminutive companions. Two years later, dressed as a girl and under the guise of a game of hide-and-seek he made a dramatic escape from London. His exile was spent with his sister Mary at the Hague and with his mother at St Germain or Paris. As he frequently quarrelled with both Henrietta Maria and his brother, Charles II, no doubt they were relieved when he found a more productive outlet for his energy and aggression as a soldier under the fine French commander, Turenne. James made a favourable impression as a military leader, even if his courage was not matched by his grasp of the finer points of strategy. In 1658 Spain was pleased to make use of his ability and experience in her war with the English Republic.

James returned to England with his brother at the time of the Restoration and was rewarded for his support with a post to which, through experience and inclination, he was well suited. He served as England's Lord High Admiral from 1660 to 1673, when an English Test Act prevented him from remaining in office. He worked hard to instill some efficiency in the service and demonstrated his customary frenetic leadership in two Dutch Wars (1665-7 and 1672-4). When in 1664 the English seized New Amsterdam from the Dutch, the king granted the colony to James, renaming it New York. Although few of the present inhabitants can be aware of it, the city and state remain to this day enduring monuments to the prince; it is curious to recall that they might just as easily have been called New Albany.

In about 1669 James made a decision which was to alter his life permanently and dramatically. He joined the Roman Catholic church, but refrained from announcing his conversion in public until 1672. In both England and Scotland the news gave rise to considerable anxiety, for in the popular imagination Catholicism was believed to foster every conceivable evil, from sorcery to sodomy. Moreover, it was associated with continual absolutism and intolerance. English worries, which had forced the Catholic Duke to surrender his position as Admiral, came to a head in the double trauma of the Popish Plot and Exclusion Crisis (1678-81). For a while there was marked political pressure for Charles to exclude his popish brother from the succession, at the height of which he twice sent James to Scotland in order to allow tempers to cool.

Despite the fact that Albany took his seat on the Privy Council without swearing the traditional oath of loyalty to king and church, his first visit to Scotland (1679-80) was uneventful. The longer second stay did not pass off so happily. James arrived late in 1680 and for a few months gave the impression of moderation. His attitude changed when he received news from England of the defeat of exclusion. The Scottish parliament was persuaded to accept him as the heir apparent, despite his religion. It also passed a Test Act making it compulsory for all officers in the church and state to take an oath accepting the 1560 Confession of Faith, upholding the royal supremacy and rejecting all covenants. Argyll (son of the earl executed by Charles II at the Restoration) was accused of treason for stating that he would accept the oath 'in so far as it was consistent with itself'. He managed to escape to Holland, however, disguised as a page bearing the train of his step-daughter. Persecution of the Covenanters was renewed, both by James and by James Drummond, Earl of Perth, his lieutenant in Scotland after his return south in 1682. Several nasty stories have come down to us of James' behaviour at this time. They may be false; they may be embellishments of minor incidents; but they do indicate the strength of feeling which the prospect of a Catholic king engendered in the minds of his subjects. Bishop Burnet relates how James delighted in watching a man being tortured by having his feet crushed to pulp in metal boots. Another tale recalls that in 1682 James was shipwrecked when returning to Scotland to collect his wife. While a henchman held off the crew and passengers, Albany bundled his strong box, dogs and Catholic priests into a lifeboat then cast off from the wreck, leaving the rest to drown.

James was never crowned in Scotland. He was the first monarch for almost 400 years not to undergo the traditional ceremony. He also never visited Scotland while he was her king. Nevertheless, so strong was the Stuart hold over their northern inheritance that there was scarcely a murmur of complaint when on 10th February 1685 the Catholic James was proclaimed king. Two months later, with obsequious loyalty but suspect historical knowledge, parliament declared that the 'solid, absolute authority' of the monarch was the 'first and fundamental law of our monarchy'. This was followed by laws making it treason to swear a covenant and death to attend a conventicle. James VII was voted a large revenue and promised a competent army. A predicted rebellion of the Covenanters was nipped in the bud by locking up many of them in Dunnottar Castle, where they suffered under dreadful overcrowded conditions. So Argyll found little support when he returned in May with a mere 300 men and urged the Scots to rise against their popish king. He was soon captured and executed after his attempt at suicide had failed. An anti-Catholic riot in Edinburgh was also swiftly quashed. At the end of the first year of his reign, therefore, James was secure and free to move on to the next stage of his policy — Catholic emancipation.

It is reckoned that at this time there were no more than about 2000 Catholics in Scotland, many of them living in isolated parts of the Highlands and Western Isles. With instinctive loyalty the Scots had accepted that the

Sir Peter Lely's portrait of James, Duke of Albany and York, the future James VII and II. The Duke was twice sent to Scotland by Charles II at the time of the English Exclusion Crisis but he did not return there as king. Inflexible, principled and obstinate, James was in many ways the very antithesis of his brother, whom he succeeded to the throne in 1685.

religion of the king might differ from their own — he was after all already a remote figure. But their toleration did not extend to the detested minority who shared the king's faith. When in 1686 James asked his second parliament (which would have done almost anything else he asked of them) to repeal the anti-Catholic laws, they refused. He was forced to rely on the royal prerogative to implement his policy. At first Catholics were permitted to worship in private houses. Then, by two Letters of Indulgence, they were freed to worship God as they wished, as long as they remained loyal. The same privilege was extended to Quakers. Finally, in June 1687 toleration was granted to Presbyterians, but not to the extremist Cameronians, who in 1688 lost their last leader, James Renwick. As well as giving Catholics freedom of worship, James elevated as many of their number as he could into important posts in his government. The positions of Chancellor and Secretary of State, for example, went to Roman Catholics.

James' policy was a failure. Toleration was interpreted by loyal episcopalians as a royal gesture of no confidence; the Presbyterians took every advantage of the new freedoms to re-establish their traditional system of worship. Naturally, they did not oppose the king who had given them so much and it was the English who eventually drove James abroad in the winter of 1688. They invited his daughter, Mary ,and her husband, William of Orange, (see family tree) to replace him. This presented the Scots with a problem. James had alienated the nobility and gentry by promoting Catholics, and the Edinburgh mob had shown its dislike of the external manifestations of royal policy by attacking the Jesuit free school and the Catholic chapel which had been set up in the nave of Holyrood Abbey. But James was still King of Scots. In St Germain he was scarcely more distant from Scotland than he had been in London. As the nation was divided, it was decided to let the estates try the matter. Representatives met William and asked him to act as a temporary executive until the estates had met in a convention parliament. This they did on 14th March 1689. The Williamites, headed by the Duke of Hamilton, were present in roughly the same numbers as the Jacobites under Claverhouse, now Viscount Dundee. The decision rested with the waverers. Both William and James had sent letters to the convention, setting out their cases. William's was considered and moderate, avoiding the thorny question of religion. The Jacobite cause was lost when James' letter was read: its curt and bitter message was simply that all Scotsmen should renew their allegiance to the king, or face the consequences. The Jacobites then made the tactical error of withdrawing from the convention. In their absence on 4th April the convention resolved that James had forfeited the throne. A ready-made alternative being to hand, a week later a delegation went south to William and Mary. The mini-interregnum ended on 11th May when William became William II of Scotland and his wife Mary II.

In vain James plotted to win back the thrones which his faith had lost him. Dundee's Highland rebellion faded away after the death of its leader at Killiecrankie, and James' personal intervention in Ireland came to an abrupt halt at the Battle of the Boyne in 1690. As other schemes either failed to get off the ground or floundered in the face of English naval superiority, the hard-pressed Louis XIV grew reluctant to waste further money on Jacobite designs. Yet the cause did not die. In Scotland there were many who remained loyal to the man they considered to be their true king, and James had a son to take up the cause after his death.

During the last few years of his life James turned with increasing devotion to the religion for which he had sacrificed his inheritance. He wrote much and prayed more, hoping, it seemed, to find greater favour with God than he had with his people. Having acquired something of the reputation of a holy man, on his death in 1701 his body was cut up and the pieces distributed to those who might appreciate them. It is strange that the Scots' College at Paris, representing a nation for whom James had shown little liking when alive, was given his brain; the English College at St Omer was granted only his bowels.

WILLIAM II AND MARY II
Joint monarchs, 1689 - 1702

William — Born: 1650. Died: 1702. Marriage: Queen Mary II. No children.

Mary — Born: 1662. Died: 1694. Marriage: William II. No children.

William II and Mary II reigned as joint monarchs of Scotland. This was the first time that such an arrangement had been used since Donald Ban and Edmund at the end of the eleventh century and, as with the previous instance, twin monarchy was adopted for purely practical reasons. Mary, as the elder daughter of the previous king, James VII and II, had a good claim to the thrones of England and Scotland. But James was still very much alive; and he also had a son. At the invitation of the disaffected aristocracy Mary's Dutch husband, William, had come over to England to maintain the Protestant ascendancy. When James VII and II fled, the English put forward the specious claim that he had thereby abdicated, thus leaving the throne vacant; the Scots, however, came up with the far more radical, but more accurate, explanation that he had forfeited the crown through his high-handed pro-Catholic policies. In the event the situation was the same both north and south of the border — the throne was there for the taking. William had left Mary behind when he invaded England. He threatened to return to Holland and his wife unless he were made at least joint sovereign with her. The English had either to accept his ultimatum or be left once more with an empty throne, which James VII and II

James VII's elder daughter Mary (seen in this elegant portrait in the style of W. Wissing) replaced her father on the Scottish throne in 1689. Married at 15 to a humourless Dutch Calvinist, William of Orange, Mary's open breach with her father caused her further unhappiness and increased her passionate dependence upon the Church of England. She knew little of Scotland or its people.

was bound to seek to recapture. Mary would not accede without her husband's consent. Thus William and Mary became joint sovereigns of England (William taking the title William III). The Scots went along with the same deal but under their own terms.

The settlement made with the new monarchs of Scotland was a form of contract. The revolution of 1688-9 destroyed once and for all the idea that the crown's power came from God and was ultimately accountable to Him alone. James VII had been expelled by the political nation because he had not ruled in its interests; the Articles of Grievances listed the various misdemeanours which the government was supposed to have perpetrated since 1660. By the Claim of Right the throne was given to William and Mary, then to Mary's sister Anne if Mary should die without issue, on condition that they upheld the traditional freedoms of the Scottish people and accepted that the monarch was under the law. William and Mary agreed to this in 1689 by swearing a new coronation oath, although William had his doubts about a clause binding him 'to root out all heretics'. He did not wish to become an instrument of factious bigotry.

The second parliament of the reign restored the Presbyterian church system on the basis of what had existed in 1592, but without episcopacy. Lay patronage of livings was also abolished, and about two-thirds of the ministers were deprived of their posts. The form of worship was that adopted by the Westminster Assembly of 1643. In the Lowlands at least, Scotland became once more a strictly Presbyterian country, dour in her faith, unforgiving in her public pronouncements. This feature of late seventeenth century Scotland is highly unattractive to a world which has recently suffered from a revival of religious intolerance. Nevertheless, there was one fortunate result of Scotland's ecclesiastical settlement: the priority given to education in Scotland from this time ensured that within a short time Scottish learning would rival that of any other European nation.

King William II was in many ways as disagreeable as the new Scottish kirk. He was a short, lean asthmatic with little sense of humour and even less sense of exuberance. He had the thin lips of an obsessive: his life was dominated by a single goal, that of saving his beloved United Dutch Provinces from the encroaching Catholic power of Louis XIV's France. William's marriage to Mary, and his acquisition of the English and Scottish thrones, were calculated to further his life's ambition. He did not necessarily agree with the limitations imposed upon him by the Scots in 1689, but at the time he accepted them for the sake of convenience. Later he infuriated his new subjects by breaking his word with impunity. He had respect for the Scots as soldiers, employing three regiments of them in his army, but he had little time for them as an independent nation. He made no secret of the fact that he believed the sooner England and Scotland joined in a full union the better it would be for both parties. He never set foot on Scottish soil.

In his personal and political life William was frugal and temperate. Bishop Burnet hinted that the king may have had homosexual inclinations, although this was unlikely because for a while he kept the squinting Elizabeth Villiers as his established mistress. Those who met William found him dull and unendurably serious-minded. Behind this reserve lay a supple, scheming mind, capable of the subtlest dissimulation. To his wife Mary he was neither kind nor faithful, although her death seemed to distress him considerably. His unhappiness might have come from a guilty conscience or, more cynically, from the upset at losing a wife popular with the subjects who so mistrusted him. She had been very useful to his cause. In battle, William was a careful but quite successful leader, capable of showing marked personal bravery in the face of continual danger. There were many plots to assassinate him. At the Battle of Neerwinden (1692), the Duke of Berwick (one of James VII's illegitimate sons by Arabella Churchill) recruited 200 hand-picked men whose sole task was to seek out William during the fighting and destroy him. William was respected as one of Europe's leading statesmen. He was an able diplomat and a fine linguist. Judged by his own standard — the preservation of the Dutch republic — his life was successful. But few Scots mourned his passing. In the spring of 1702 his favourite horse, Sorel, stumbled over a mole hill in the grounds of Hampton Court, throwing the king to the ground and breaking his collar bone. Although the injury was not serious, he developed pleurisy and died. He was buried at night with simple Calvinist obsequies.

William and Mary were cousins. Apart from descent from Charles I they had little else in common. Mary was 12 years younger than William, a devout Anglican, an inveterate chatterer and a naive politician. She wept for more than 24 hours when she was told that a marriage had been arranged for her with William III of Orange, the taciturn Dutch weakling. Well might she have sobbed at her fate, for her husband proved to be not only physically unattractive but showed little interest in her. Their union was childless. The lonely princess found solace in religion and in later life she made pathetic gestures against what she believed to be the lax morality prevailing among the English upper classes. She remained obsessively loyal to William and, although painfully lacking in confidence, she did her best to oversee the government of Britain when he was away on campaign in the summer months.

When they were married in 1677, William had already been Stadholder (chief executive), Captain General and Admiral General of the United Provinces for five years. The first 12 years of their life together were spent in Holland. The circumstances of their return to England, which involved Mary replacing her father on the throne, weighed heavily on her conscience. She died of smallpox in 1694, alienated from her father, at odds with her sister, Anne, and never having established much of a relationship with William. She had little influence on English affairs, less on Scottish. In fact, as far as Scotland was concerned, she might as well not have existed.

Despite the attempts to limit royal authority in the 1689-90 Settlement, William governed Scotland much as his two predecessors had done, through a Secretary of State for Scotland in London and a Commissioner acting on his behalf in Edinburgh. Scottish ministers were particularly irked at having to go south on occasion to seek favours from William's Dutch favourites, such as the Earl of Portland. The extent of William's concern for Scottish affairs may be gathered from a remark he made towards the end of his reign when he was detained in London by pressing business from his northern kingdom:

> ...what vexes me in particular is that this affair retards my departure for Holland, for which I long more than ever.

In the late 1690s the king's patent lack of concern for all matters Scottish, except when they interfered with his Dutch business, made it more difficult for the Scots to stomach the twin hardships of terrible harvests and a downturn in trade. It is estimated that together they reduced one in six Scots to beggary. Obviously the Dutchman could not be held responsible for natural disasters, but his dragging Scotland into the continental war against Louis XIV certainly damaged commercial enterprise. In Scottish eyes he was also personally responsible for two further tragedies which beset the nation during his troubled reign.

Scotland was not won for William and Mary without a fight from the Jacobites, those still loyal to James VII. The Duke of Gordon held Edinburgh Castle until June 1689 and Patrick Stewart, Marquis of Atholl, also defended Blair Castle for a while. The most serious threat to the new regime came from Dundee, a soldier who had fought on the continent for William; it was rumoured that on one occasion he had saved the Stadholder's life. 'Bonny Dundee' raised a powerful force of Highlanders, mighty in the charge but low on discipline, with which he managed to ambush the Williamite forces under General MacKay in the pass of Killiecrankie. Two thousand government troops were lost as they struggled with the new-fangled bayonets, swept aside by the yelling, half-naked hoard which careered down upon them from the slopes of the narrow defile. But Dundee fell in the mêlée. Without his leadership the Jacobite cause was severely handicapped. In August the rebels were defeated at Dunkeld by a new regiment of Cameronians, no doubt keen to revenge themselves for the bullying of the 'Highland host'. The next year the Jacobites met with a final reverse at Cromdale. To control the Highlands, MacKay built Fort William, a daunting symbol of the new regime, and in 1691 a general pardon was wisely granted to all rebels. The story, however, did not end there.

The events of the Massacre of Glencoe are simply told. An explanation of events is much less accessible. The government demanded that by New Year's Day 1692 all Highland chiefs take an oath of allegiance to the new regime. Alasdair MacDonald of Glencoe, the venerable leader of a small branch of his clan, did not swear until 6th January, partly as a result of his own late arrival and partly because when he did turn up there was no official present to administer the oath. The government decided to make an example of him. Argyll troops with Campbell officers, under the overall command of the inadequate Captain Robert Campbell, were stationed with the MacDonalds on 1st February. On the 12th they received orders to extirpate their hosts. The next day 38 MacDonalds were slain (among whom were two women and two children), their homes were destroyed and more than 100 survivors fled to the icy winter hills where many perished for want of food and shelter. MacDonald and his wife were killed in the initial onslaught. The history of the Highlands is thick with tales of murder, deceit and brutality. But the events in Glencoe were received with universal horror and condemnation, not only in Scotland but in England and wherever else the story was related. Acting under government command the troops had broken the age-old rules of hospitality, which meant much more than we may imagine in an age without motor cars and motels. In enlightened circles, official brutality was no longer regarded as acceptable; when coupled with deceit and the deaths of women and children it provoked outrage. William's reputation in Scotland was so deeply stained by the gore of Glencoe that no conciliatory measure ever succeeded in cleansing it.

But was William to blame? The hatred between the Campbells and the MacDonalds went back to the time when the latter were deprived of the Lordship of the Isles, and the clans had been ranged against each other during the civil wars earlier in the century. The hand of a Campbell was to be found at almost every stage of the Glencoe tragedy: the Sheriff-Depute who should have been present to hear Alasdair MacDonald's oath on 2nd January was Campbell of Ardkinglas (he was in fact suffering from a hangover after a heavy Hogmanay); the Campbell Earl of Breadalbane urged William to sign the extirpation order; and Campbells commanded the troops who carried out the slaughter. Responsibility for the policy of forcibly bringing the Highlands to heel, of which the massacre was but a part, lay with Sir John Dalrymple, Master of Stair; he must bear considerable responsibility for what happened. Although blood-feuds were common in the Highlands, it was not for the king to encourage or exploit them. Ultimately it is the head of a government who must answer for its actions: William signed the order for murder in the glen. He knew of Dalrymple's scheme, and if he was not sure exactly what was in the paper at the time he signed it, then it was his duty to have found out before adding his name. Not until 1695 did he grant an enquiry into what had happened.

The sorry trail of misunderstanding, villainy and bad luck which led to the Glencoe massacre crumpled William's reputation. It did not seriously harm the bulk of the Scottish nation. However, towards the end of the reign, an event occurred which proved a serious economic setback to thousands of Scots and confirmed beyond doubt the tarnished reputation which they had already loaded upon their alien king.

In the late seventeenth century Scotland remained one of the very poorest nations in Europe. Enterprising Scots found this especially irksome at a time when England was emerging as a country of power and fortune, particularly through her canny and ruthless exploitation of colonial markets. Although lacking the expertise, as well as the military and financial back up, the Scots determined to do something about their plight by founding a trading colony of their own in the New World. The place they selected was Darien on the Isthmus of Panama. A quick glance at the map will reveal that the site was in several ways well chosen, not least because it formed a convenient link and entrepôt between Pacific and Atlantic trade. On the other hand the would-be colonisers might have asked themselves why, two centuries after Columbus had first reached the West Indies, no major power had yet established a base on the Isthmus. The Spanish laid claim to the territory but had no presence there. The first Scottish convoy sailed from Leith in 1698 with four ships and 1500 men. When it arrived at its destination, the pioneers soon discovered why others had been loath to settle the district. Accustomed to the abrasive Scottish climate, the explorers found the unrelenting tropical heat and humidity distressingly ennervating. Malaria, tuberculosis and yellow fever killed hundreds and incapacitated many more. Spanish harassment finished the colony off. Humiliated and bitter, the miserable remnants of three proud expeditions returned home in 1700. Responsibility for the failure of the Darien scheme must rest principally with those who had organised it. They knew that they would face Spanish and English hostility, and they could have reconnoitred the terrain more carefully. But national esteem had taken a terrible blow. Two thousand settlers had died and most of the £400,000 raised (equivalent to almost the total value of the kingdom's coinage) had been lost. At times of disaster men seek a scapegoat.

Lobbied by the East India Company, the English parliament had ensured that the Scottish colonial adventure would always be short of capital by forbidding any Englishmen to invest in it. Moreover, the king banned English settlers and vessels from aiding the sufferers at Darien. When the Scottish enterprise was launched William was trying to remain on good terms with Spain, to prevent Louis XIV from extending his influence into the peninsula. As the childless Charles II of Spain was on the point of death (a position he had obstinately maintained throughout most of his painful life), William was desperate to see that the lands of the vast Spanish empire did not fall into the hands of France. In refusing to help the Darien project William was predictably placing the interests of Holland and the European anti-French alliance before those of the Scots. There might have been a tactful way round the problem, but if there was William was not prepared to look for it. When news of the Darien disaster reached Scotland the nation was smitten with a wave of anglophobia. In Edinburgh riots were directed against William personally. It was when he heard of these that the king complained of Scottish affairs keeping him from returning to Holland for a while. At the time there were many Scots who felt that it would have been better for them had he never left the Low Countries in the first place.

ANNE
1702 - 1707/14

Born: 1665. Died: 1714. Marriage: Prince George of Denmark. Children: William, George, Mary, Anne, Mary and 13 other stillbirths or miscarriages.

Queen Anne was the last monarch of an independent Scotland. She visited the country once, when her father (James Duke of Albany, the future James VII) was in exile there at the time of the English exclusion crisis, and she spent her seventeenth birthday in Edinburgh. This was an unhappy time for her, not because she disliked Scotland or her folk — although she did later confess to finding the Scots a 'strange people' — but because she witnessed religious bigotry at first hand. She was horrified by her father's intensely cruel persecution of the remaining covenanters. The experience was to have two important influences on her future thinking: she was prepared to desert James in 1688 when his Catholicism alienated him from the English political nation and threatened to cast England into civil war, and she became a firm believer, as had all monarchs since the time of James VI and I, in the need for a full and complete union of the northern and southern kingdoms. After she left Scotland in 1682, 140 years were to elapse before the country was again graced by the presence of her monarch (excluding, of course, the Jacobite pretenders). When George IV visited Scotland in 1822 he did so not as King of Scotland but as King of Great Britain.

Anne was the second daughter of the Duke of Albany's first marriage. Not much is known of her childhood. As was the custom at that time, she was removed from her mother shortly after birth and given to a wet nurse. She lived apart from her parents at Richmond Palace, and her mother's death in 1671 does not appear to have upset her unduly. Her education was hardly suitable for a future queen but it was no worse than that given to most well-born young ladies of the age; music and languages were prominent, history largely ignored. Far more important than any formal training were the lessons in survival which Anne picked up as she went along. Stories of the civil wars and her grandfather's execution abounded. In her own lifetime she witnessed the turmoils and vicissitudes of a precariously mutable political scene both in Britain and abroad. She was continually reminded of the proximity of death by her own physical weakness, and the tragic early demise of her children and many members of her family. Although she was by nature somewhat stubborn and conservative, the effect of these experiences on her intelligent mind was to sow seeds of pragmatism, enabling her to realise that the highest principle in the world is of little worth on the lips of a severed head, and of scarcely greater value in the mind of a deposed king.

There was a time when Anne was caricatured as a vast, tea-taking, card-playing nonenity with lesbian tendencies. As scholarship over the last 50 or so years has revealed, such an image does her a gross injustice. She was somewhat unoriginal yet possessed of an acute understanding and a strong sense of duty. Her only contribution of any note to the history of Scotland was the urging of the union with England. This she did not in a spirit of colonialism or imperialism, but as a reasonably dispassionate observer she honestly believed that the proposal would benefit both countries. Those who believe its effects have proved otherwise do Anne an injustice if they blame her for this.

Anne was a handsome young girl. She had a comely figure, dark brown hair, a full, slightly sad face and celebrated fine hands. At the age of 12 she was permanently scarred by smallpox. All her life she suffered from acute myopia which made her feel uncomfortable in large crowded gatherings and caused her to frown when looking towards anyone entering her presence. The unfortunate impression this created can easily be guessed at. Unlike her sister she was not a great talker, although her voice was attractive. A rather wicked sense of humour can be discerned from the nickname (Caliban) she gave to her humourless and mean-looking brother-in-law, William II.

At the age of 18 Anne married the 30-year-old Prince George of Denmark, the brother of King Christian V. He was 'a handsome fine gentleman', fair haired, large and military. Those who knew him well found an open, kindly man to whom Anne was devoted. To be sure, some of this devotion stemmed from the fact that from the start she ruled the household, leaving genial George to trot around behind her. When war broke out in 1702 he was flattered with the splendid title 'Generalissimo', which in fact meant nothing. The nation's destiny could not very well be left in the hands of a man who 'is very fat, loves news, his bottle, and the queen'. Perceptive to the point of cruelty, Charles II summed him up best: 'I have tried him drunk and I have tried him sober, and there is nothing in him.' More patient in her search, Anne found a kind heart, and that is all she needed.

The queen never enjoyed good health. Indeed, in later life rheumatism rendered her a virtual invalid so that she had to go hunting in a kind of chariot, careering about the countryside like some form of gouty middle-aged Boadicea. A Scottish commissioner described her in 1707 as 'the most despicable mortal I had ever seen in any station', with a 'red and spotted' face, 'negligent dress' and in 'extream pain and agony'. After George's death in 1708, predeceased by all her 18 children, Anne was not only sick but also entirely alone.

The Scottish parliament unanimously recognised Anne as their queen in June 1702. The new monarch was never crowned in Scotland and her coronation medal, engraved with the tactless phrase 'Entirely English' (to distinguish her from her foreign predecessor, William II and III), cannot have endeared her to the subjects of her northern realm. Nevertheless, she subsequently gave Scotland much of her attention, reestablishing the ancient Order of the Thistle in 1703 and following carefully the proceedings in the Scottish parliament. She was personally present in the English parliament when union was under discussion. In the spring of 1707 she delayed her annual retreat to Windsor in order to see the Act of Union safely through. Not everyone agreed with the measure, but Scotland certainly suffered many monarchs less genuinely solicitous of the nation's welfare than Anne, the last of the Stuarts.

THE ACT OF UNION 1707

The independent Scottish monarchy, which over the years had been preserved in the face of English aggression at such enormous cost, was cut off at a stroke by the 1707 Act of Union. To Scottish nationalists the Union was the supreme betrayal; to pragmatists it represented the natural culmination of a process which had begun with the Union of the Crowns in 1603. What is most remarkable, however, is the suddenness with which the amalgamation of the two countries took place.

Anglo-Scottish relations had been poor throughout the seventeenth century. Scots had ranged themselves against the government in England at the time of the Covenant, and with the Engagement signed with Charles I in 1647. They had been subjected to Cromwellian conquest in the 1650s. Hostility persisted during the reigns of Charles II and James VII, and the settlement which Scotland made with William II in 1689-90 gave the country a greater degree of independence than it had enjoyed since the time of James VI. The breach with England was widened further by the Glencoe massacre, the failure of the Darien scheme and the economic blight which settled on the country in the 1690s. By the beginning of Anne's reign it appeared more likely that the two kingdoms would split apart than fuse together. So what made the union possible?

Schemes for uniting the whole of Britain into a single country had been put forward in 1606, 1667, 1670 and 1689, but each time they had been wrecked on the rocks of racism and fear. There was a feeling among the English that 'whoever married a beggar cou'd only exspect a louse for a portion' — in other words, there was no material benefit for them in the plans for union. For their part, the Scots were anxious not to be swallowed up by their more prosperous, populous and powerful southern neighbour. The change of heart came first from the English government. In 1702 it found itself once more at war with the France of Louis XIV. The Sun King had recognised the Catholic James VIII, 'the Young Pretender' (son of the exiled James VII), as the rightful heir to both the Scottish and English thrones. Especially among Highlanders and episcopalians,

A charming portrait by William Wissing of the 21-year-old Anne who, by signing the 1707 Act of Union, became the last monarch of an independent Scotland. She believed fervently that the economic and political benefits of union would far outweigh problem incurred by the loss of national independence.

there were many in Scotland who felt sympathetic towards the Jacobite cause. Indeed, had James VIII moved sharply in 1702 and landed in Scotland to claim his throne he might well have been accepted by the Scots instead of Anne. As it was, the 14-year-old pretender, blessed with as hopeless a sense of timing as his father, did nothing. When Anne's son and heir died in 1701 the English parliament responded swiftly with an Act of Settlement. In the likely event of Anne dying childless it passed the succession to Sophia of Hanover, a cousin of Charles I (see family tree). The Scots would not go along with this. After abortive discussions on union in 1702-3 their parliament passed a number of acts hostile to England, chief among which was the Act of Security. This gave the Scottish parliament the right to nominate a successor to Anne within 20 days of her death; the nominee was not necessarily to be from the House of Hanover. This raised the prospect of Scotland once more having her own independent monarchy. It was not this that terrified the English so much as the threat of a revival of the Auld Alliance between Scotland and France, bringing with it the possibility of Jacobite invasion and civil war at a time when the country was already stretched to the limit by the War of Spanish Succession (1702-1713). Moreover, the English army relied heavily upon the doughty Scottish soldiers in its ranks; it did not relish the prospect of seeing them lined up with the French. When Anne hesitated to sign the Act of Security, the Scottish parliament withheld supply until she succumbed to their demand.

Thus by the middle of 1704 we find Scottish politicians making the first tentative steps towards complete independence from England, while Anne and her English government were trying to bind the two nations more closely. The queen's ill-health made some sort of speedy settlement essential. In theory the Scots held the whip hand. Their failure to exploit the situation can be put down to their own disunity and the superior economic strength of the English. First, pressure was put on the Scots with the Alien Act of February 1705. This gave the Scots until Christmas Day to accept the Hanoverian succession or appoint commissioners to negotiate a union. If they did neither, Scots would be treated as aliens in England (threatening all their property held there), and their trade with England and her colonies would be destroyed. The economic consequences of this on Scotland would have been disastrous. There was no way that closer ties with France could compensate for loss of English business. At the same time English money was made freely available for Scottish MPs if they would support the plans for union. There is some truth in Burns' claim that his countrymen were 'bought and sold for English gold'. A snap vote in a poorly attended Scottish parliament agreed to the commissioners who would negotiate the union being appointed by the queen. Discussions began in April 1706 and were completed with few problems by the middle of July. There were roars of protest when the terms of the proposed union were published, but the Scottish parliament accepted them by a considerable majority on 16th January 1707. It had in effect voted itself out of existence. With poignant litotes Chancellor Seafield wistfully observed: 'Now there's ane end of ane old song.' The last

Scottish parliament was dissolved by the last Scottish monarch on 28th April 1707.

By the terms of the Act of Union England and Scotland became one country. Anne became Queen of Great Britain with the succession going to Hanover on her death. There was full economic union, with free trade and the same customs levies on either side of the border. The Scots were granted 45 seats in the House of Commons and 16 peers in the upper house. This was not a fair reflexion of the population difference between the two countries (England five million, Scotland one million), but it was justified by pointing out that the Scottish contribution to the total revenue of the nation was proportionately much lower than the imbalance in population. The terms of the union were made easier for the Scots to swallow by the gift of an 'Equivalent' of £398,085-10s (English), a compensation for agreeing to share responsibility for England's national debt. The money was intended for those who had lost through the Darien scheme. It was really little more than a bribe.

It is quite clear why the English government and parliament wanted union. For the first time in their history they were entering upon the European stage as a major military power — the Duke of Marlborough had scored the first of his astonishing victories against the French at Blenheim in 1704 and followed it up with another at Ramillies two years later. The last thing his government wanted was trouble on the home front. However high it might be in financial terms, the cost of union had to be met in order to acquire strategic security. But why had the Scots agreed to so unequal a marriage in which they were bound to be the junior partner? Nationalist advocates of divorce say the country was sold, lured into a shoddy partnership by the size of the dowry. There is an element of truth in this: individual bribes and the Equivalent certainly did help some Scots to control their nationalism. But there were other less obscene forces at work. The union did not touch the Scottish legal system or the kirk. For the latter the union offered security in its dominant position. The new arrangement also brought political stability at a time when Scotland was dangerously divided between Highlands and Lowlands. It cannot have been completely forgotten that the Cromwellian union, however much it might have bruised national pride, enabled the country to enjoy an almost unprecedented spate of domestic tranquility. Finally, there were the merchant classes who hoped that access to English markets, particularly those in the New World, would present Scottish entrepreneurs with grand opportunities for commercial expansion. The arguments they put forward were not unlike those urged today in favour of membership of the European Community.

If there had been an easy way of unilaterally undoing the union the Scots would have certainly have taken it at some time during the first 50 years of its existence. In 1713 they pressed the issue in parliament with some success. However, as long as the majority of English MPs felt the union to be to their advantage there was no way that the handful of Scottish MPs could break it. The only alternative — armed insurrection — never found wide appeal.

The Scottish Privy Council was abolished in 1708 (in clear contravention of the spirit of the previous year's understanding). This left Scotland with little national administration. This was the chief drawback of the union and swiftly led many Scots to believe that their worst fears were being realised, and that their country was becoming little more than a poor northern appendix of England. These anxieties were fed by a number of Acts, such as that establishing the same treason laws for both England and Scotland (thereby undermining the independence of the Scottish judiciary), and the 1712 Toleration Act which granted greater freedom to Scottish episcopalians. Even the Equivalent was suspect: promised hard cash, the Scots had been horrified to find the bulk of it paid in dubious-looking English Exchequer Bills. The serious mob riots in Glasgow in 1724 and in Edinburgh 12 years later were essentially anglophobic in inspiration.

Yet the union survived. Gradually the Scottish economy picked up, although it is impossible to say to what extent this was due to the effects of the revolution of 1707. Agriculture was modernised. Glasgow became one of the great British merchant cities. And the Scots did not lose their sense of national identity. The influence they exercised over Britain as a whole was far greater than might be expected from their tiny population. In 1707 an old song did indeed come to its end. But it was soon replaced by several others, not all of them laments.

Louis Blanchet's fine picture of the Young Pretender, the elder son of 'James VIII' and better known as Bonnie Prince Charlie. Although a good-looking and charming young man, his character was seriously flawed and he had insufficient military experience for the daring assault on Britain which he undertook in 1745.

THE JACOBITES
1689 - 1807

The exiled House of Stuart tried on several occasions to win back the crowns they had lost in 1688-9. Although their efforts all ended in failure, at the time they were seen as a very real threat, particularly when they were involved in armed insurrection on the British mainland.

JACOBITISM

On 4th April 1689 a convention parliament declared that James VII had forfeited the Scottish throne. Legally speaking, the pronouncement was dubious. In theory parliaments had to be summoned by the monarch, so the very existence of the convention was of suspect constitutionality. Even if it had been properly summoned it had no power to dismiss a king who sat on the throne through inherited right. The English got round the problem by claiming that James II (as they knew him) had fled, thereby abdicating the throne. Since the king had never set foot in Scotland since his accession, a similar declaration in the northern kingdom would have been rather less convincing. Mary Queen of Scots had been removed, but only by persuading her to abdicate. There is no way that James was going to follow her unfortunate example. So what in fact the Scots engineered in 1689 was a revolution. Despite all the mystique of coronation and the centuries-old tradition of hereditary monarchy, the king was removed because he did not please those with greater political power. It was a blatant act of realpolitik. Needless to say, it was unacceptable to James and a considerable number of his erstwhile subjects.

The supporters of the exiled James VII, his son 'James VIII', and grandsons 'Charles III' and 'Henry IX', are known as Jacobites. The word comes from Jacobus, the Latin for James. Jacobitism is as controversial and emotive a topic today as it was 250 years ago. Professional historians are divided about how much support the movement had and, consequently, about how real a threat it was to the British establishment. Moreover, the story of the Jacobites has been romanticised over the years. There were followers of the exiled Stuarts in England and Ireland, but it was in Scotland that they were at their strongest and where they fought most doggedly for their cause. They believed that William II, Mary II and Anne had been imposed on the Scots by the English and that the 1707 Act of Union was the inevitable child of this forced marriage. Thus Jacobitism became inextricably intertwined with Scottish nationalism. Not only was it the cause of a deprived royal family; in the imagination of many it was the cause of a downtrodden and exploited nation. To drink a toast to the 'king over the water' became a defiant gesture of Scottish independence. It was all too easily forgotten that it was the Stuarts who had moved the Scottish court to London and ruled their original kingdom as absentee monarchs for over a century before the union.

The Jacobite drama had three principal characters and a large supporting cast. It unfolded in several acts. In the first James VII held the centre of the stage. Upon his death in 1701 his place went to his son 'James VIII' (1688-1766), the Old Pretender. In the middle of the eighteenth century he was upstaged by his son Bonnie Prince Charlie (1720-1780), who after his father's death called himself 'Charles III'. Cardinal Henry Benedict Stuart, brother of the prince, provided a rather downbeat epilogue and the performance ended in silence with his death in 1807.

During the reign of James VII the Jacobites made several attempts to recapture the throne. The first, and only one which properly concerns Scotland, has been dealt with under the story of William and Mary. In 1690 the king himself landed in Ireland but was crushed at the Battle of the Boyne and retired to France. Two years later an invasion fleet which the French had assembled for him was defeated by the English in the Bay of la Hogue. This was the second time that a Stuart monarch had been thwarted by a navy which he had spent time and money building into an effective fighting force. Charles I had angered his English subjects by collecting for the navy a tax known as Ship Money, only to find the service ranged against him in the civil war which broke out in 1642. As Lord High Admiral, James Duke of York and Albany had also worked hard to increase the strength of the navy, which then smashed his hopes of making a comeback in 1692. 'James VIII' made three attempts to get to Britain. In 1708 a fleet reached the Firth of Forth but retired when it found little evidence of support. A full-scale Jacobite rising took place in 1715. It was ill-timed and James arrived too late to provide it with the much needed figurehead. The Old Pretender's last venture occurred four years later. Backed by Spanish rather than French troops, it achieved even less that the 1715 rebellion. There were several plots against the Hanoverian government, many of which were more or less Jacobite inspired. They came to nothing. The final Jacobite assault was the famous '45 rebellion of Prince Charles. The overwhelming defeat at Culloden in 1746 finished it and the cause of the exiled Stuarts for ever.

The Jacobites were a mixed bag of malcontents. They included Roman Catholics and others dissatisfied with the dominance of the kirk. Many Highlanders were attracted to the cause, fired either by a vague sense of resentment at the inexorable encroachment into their glens of English and Lowland ways, or by the age-old thirst for plunder. Some Scots disillusioned at the results of the 1707 union were drawn to the Stuart standard, as were English Tories who had been left out in the cold when George I succeeded to the throne in 1714. Many made sweeping declarations of Jacobite sympathy when there was little chance of being called upon to honour them, only to experience a rapid change of heart when faced with the prospect of losing all they possessed, even their lives, when a Pretender called them to arms. As a contemporary sneered, they were 'Jacobites when drunk, Hanoverians when sober'.

Explanations of Jacobite failure are numerous. At the time the threat to Britain was taken with deadly seriousness and there was nothing inevitable about its defeat. Individual misfortunes can be explained by an unhappy confluence of ill-luck, indecision, poor leadership and internal wrangling. To have any realistic chance of success the Jacobites probably needed substantial continental backing. This was never forthcoming. Time and again a vicious circle was drawn in which the Jacobites refused to rise unless supported by professional troops, while continental governments were unwilling to commit troops to the movement until it gave evidence of its sincerity and popularity by organising a significant rebellion. The growing prosperity of southern Scotland as the century progressed bonded Lowlanders more tightly to the government. Their hearts might not have lain with their Hanoverian gold, but at least their minds did. In Scotland, therefore, Jacobitism became a divided cause in a divided nation. For some 60 years it was the dominant feature of Highland history and when it was eventually destroyed on Culloden Field, traditional Highland culture perished with it. Anthropologists and fantasists have mourned this double passing. Strangely, the two corpses have attracted far more sympathy than was ever lavished upon the living bodies.

'JAMES VIII'
Pretender to the throne 1701-1766

Born: 1688. Died: 1766. Marriage: Princess Maria Clementina Sobieska. Children: Charles and Henry.

The birth of James Francis Edward Stuart on 10 June 1688 cost his father his throne. There were many in England who were prepared to tolerate the high-handed Catholic policies of James II as long as there was no chance of their continuing after the king's death. However, the unexpected birth of a son opened up the dismal prospect of an unending line of Catholic monarchs and spurred the discontented aristocracy into treasonous rebellion. The king fled, and was declared to have abdicated. His son was proclaimed an impostor, smuggled into the queen's bed in a warming pan as she lay in real or feigned labour. From the very day of his birth, therefore, James Francis found himself rejected by his subjects. The circumstances of his birth became the subject of a derisive nursery rhyme, 'Rock-a-bye-baby'.

James was given a remarkable number of nicknames during the course of

L. G. Blanchet's portrait of the dignified 'James VIII', the Old Pretender. The nearest James came to the Scottish crown was during the Jacobite rebellion of 1715, but he arrived too late to play much of a part in the proceedings and returned to his continental exile after only a few brief weeks in Scotland.

his life, each of which throws light on his career and personality. Although he was initially known as the Warming Pan Baby, he grew up to acquire a more favourable sobriquet, the 'Bonnie Black Laddie'. This referred to his dark good looks. He was tall and quite athletic, with his mother's raven hair and black eyes. During the early years of the eighteenth century the major states of western Europe were taken up with the War of Spanish Succession, fought upon the death of the last Spanish Habsburg monarch, Charles II, to determine who should control Spain and her massive overseas empire. As James had been brought up in France and looked to her king, Louis XIV, for assistance in regaining his kingdoms, it was fitting that he should do what he could to help Louis in his ambition of seeing a Bourbon on the Spanish throne. The supposedly anonymous 'Chevalier de Saint George' served with some distinction among Louis' household troops at the battles of Oudenarde and Malplaquet (1708 and 1709). Yet before he became known as the Chevalier, James had picked up another, less flattering name, the Pretender.

When James VII died on 6th September 1701 Louis promptly ordered a herald to proclaim in English, French and Latin, that 'James VIII' was now king of England, Scotland and Ireland. When a similar ceremony was attempted in London it was broken up by a scornful mob. To all but the Jacobites, James was a mere Pretender. Nevertheless, he was quite hopeful of winning back the inheritance his father had lost. Had not his uncle, Charles II, successfully recovered his throne after many years in continental exile? The youthful James saw no reason why he should not do likewise. Charles, prepared to promise almost anything if he thought it might make his life easier, had been invited back on the strength of the chimerical declaration he made at Breda. As Anne reminded him, James had the opportunity to make a similar gesture of reconciliation, one that would almost certainly enable him to return to his kingdom on the death of Anne. All he had to do was renounce his Catholicism. But this James was never prepared to do. So the years passed and expectation turned into hope, then finally into a dream which he knew he could never realise.

In 1704 the Jacobites hatched the rather feeble Scots Plot. The next year James and Louis began preparations for an altogether more ambitious scheme. Nathaniel Hooke was twice sent to sound out public opinion in Scotland and returned each time to report that the arrival of James would be greeted with the utmost cordiality. Since anglophobia was now at its height, there was probably a good deal of truth in what Hooke had to say. The expedition did not set sail from Dunkirk until March 1708, delayed by French hesitation, incompetence among the Jacobites and their allies, and finally by James catching measles ('Old Mr Misfortune' he was later to be called — the name could just as easily have been applied to almost any of the Stewarts). Once at sea ill-luck sailed with him. Admiral Fourbin failed to make the rendezvous with the Jacobites on the Firth of Forth, the weather turned nasty and a superior English squadron under the skillful admiral Byng forced the Jacobites to retire. The Pretender had pleaded in vain with Fourbin to be put ashore, alone if necessary, to try his hand at rallying the Scottish people. After a brief sortie towards Inverness, in early April the little armada returned battered and dispirited to Dunkirk. Louis XIV had bade farewell to James as he left for his expedition with a rather backhanded expression of good luck: 'The best I can wish you is that I may never see your face again.' The hope was unfulfilled. James' increasingly mournful visage was to haunt Louis for several years to come.

A king without a kingdom is also a king without subjects and without provision. This was James' besetting problem. He was dependent upon the charity of others for his subsistence and the wherewithal for his enterprises. A proposed second French invasion in 1710 came to nothing. Three years later War of Spanish Succession was over as far as Anglo-French hostilities were concerned. A clause in the Treaty of Utrecht (1713) stipulated that the Pretender was to reside in France no longer. 'Jamie the Rover' retired to Bar-le-Duc in Lorraine. From here communications with British Jacobites and forces on the French coast were at best problematic. The isolation of the Chevalier grew.

The death of Queen Anne in 1714 and the succession of 'a wee German lairdie' to the British throne presented James with an excellent opportunity to try for the crown once more. As Anne's reign drew to a close a number of leading Tory politicians had professed Jacobite sympathies, so there was quite a well of support for James to draw on. Again, the problem was one of timing. He was not able to mobilise support in 1714, thereby giving the new dynasty time to calm some of the wilder xenophobic fears harboured by the British people. And when the revolt did come, James all but missed it.

The 1715 Jacobite rebellion began at Braemar on 26th August with a gathering that was ostensibly part of a deer hunt. The revolt became public on 6th September with the raising of the standard of 'King James VIII' by an ex-Secretary of State for Scotland and former unionist, John Erskine, sixth Earl of Mar. The earl's sense of timing was unfortunate: of the two men essential for the rebellion's success, one — Louis XIV — had died five days previously, the other — 'King' James himself — was on the other side of Europe. Adopting various disguises, the Pretender made his way across France as swiftly as he could to the coast at St Malo. Here the tall, gloomy-looking man, who sometimes appeared as a bishop, sometimes as a servant or sailor, tried in vain to find a vessel to take him to Scotland. At the end of the year he found his secret way north to Dunkirk, boarded a frigate, and arrived at Peterhead in Aberdeenshire three days before Christmas. Maintaining his theatrically transparent incognito he joined George Keith, Earl Marshal, at Newburgh. James then moved south to link up with 'Bobbing John' Mar, whose progress over the previous four months had not been exactly thrilling. As many as 12,000 men had responded to his call. It was ominous, though, that those who best knew the cautious and scheming earl were the least willing to come forward. Their misgivings were well founded. It quickly became apparent that Mar was no military leader and had little idea what to do next. Perth fell to the Jacobites, but Stirling and Edinburgh held fast. A paltry force of Lowlanders and Northumberland gentry made a sortie into Lancashire, where they were forced to surrender at Preston on 14th November. The previous day Mar's Jacobites had met greatly outnumbered government troops under the Earl of Argyll on Sheriffmuir. Although both sides claimed to have won, it was the Hanoverians who remained in the field at the end of the muddled conflict. Time was running out for Mar and his men. The Highlanders began to slink off back to their glens with their plunder. No help was forthcoming from the French government, now in the hands of the Duke of Orleans who was eager to preserve the Utrecht settlement. In England the government's forces were reinforced with thousands more professional troops from the continent. Into this cheerless scenario had stepped the Pretender.

Over Christmas and New Year 1715-16 'James VIII' held court at Scone. A coronation was planned and Jacobite ladies persuaded to hand over their jewels for fashioning into a crown. What sort of man was it the Scots were preparing to honour in this way? James looked and carried himself like a king. He was brave, sincere and honest. Moreover, he did not display the religious bigotry of his father. Although unflinchingly Catholic, he professed no wish to see his religion enforced upon his subjects; he was without crusading zeal. But that was precisely the problem. James was about as charismatic as a haggis. At a time when the fate of the Jacobite cause hung in the balance, his supporters turned to him for inspiration and uplift, determination and encouragement. They found not one of these qualities in the introverted and depressed young man who paced silently round the cold corridors of Scone with a face like the heavy northern sky. When asked if he considered the outlook bleak, he concurred, adding with Eeyore-like gloom: 'It is no new thing for me to be unfortunate'. One of his company recorded: 'We saw nothing in him that looked like spirit ... Our men began to despise him; some asked if he could speak.'

With their numbers diminishing all the time, in January the Jacobites withdrew north over the frozen waters of the Tay. By the time they reached Montrose their army had literally disintegrated. James, Mar and a small entourage went aboard a French vessel lying in the harbour and set sail for France. After a brief detour along the Norwegian coast to avoid the Royal Navy, they put in to Gravelines on 10th February. The Pretender wrote a tactless letter to those who had risked their lives in his cause, saying that he had fled to France for their own good. He never returned to Scotland.

Foiled once more in an attempt to secure a permanent home, 'the Rover' now moved south, first to Avignon then in 1717 to Rome. From here he continued to plot with anyone who might be prepared to consider helping him. He even approached the illustrious Charles XII of Sweden, who had his own quarrel with the Hanoverians. But the great general was killed before anything could come of the plan. The next year a more exciting prospect opened up when James was approached by the government of Philip V of Spain. With unaccustomed alacrity James travelled to Madrid, where he was established in his own palace. He found that two expeditions were planned, the larger of which was quite a formidable undertaking, involving 5000 men and arms for a further 30,000. But the precedent for Spanish armadas was not good. Before it reached British waters the fleet was broken up by storms in the Bay of Biscay. This left only a small force of about 300 men under George Keith, Earl Marishal, and William Murray, Marquis of Tullibardine, to make its way in two frigates to Stornoway in Lewis. The Pretender was not with them, which was probably just as well for morale of the rebels and, as it turned out, for James himself. The leaders did not see eye to eye, their arsenal at Eilean Donan was captured by the navy and on 10th September they were defeated at Glenshiel. Small wonder that the Chevalier was now coming to be known as 'Old Mr Melancholy'.

Later that year something occurred that should have brought a smile even to James' mournful lips. The 31-year-old prince was married to the attractive 16-year-old grand-daughter of the king of Poland, Maria Clemtina Sobieska. She was vivacious, lively and bright — an ideal tonic, many thought, for the depressed Pretender. But opposites do not always complement each other. The marriage was a disaster. The couple squabbled bitterly over the education of their two sons, Charles Edward and Henry Benedict. Maria also criticised James' choice of friends and advisors and she disapproved of the way he behaved with them. When relations between the ill-matched pair became impossible Maria retired to a convent for a while. She died in 1735, weakened by her religious excesses and exhausted by constant struggle with her dull but obstinate husband.

An air of profound dejection now hung over the Roman court of the Old Pretender (so called since the arrival of a son in 1720). The Pope ensured that James had enough money to live in reasonable style but when the pontiff ordered, with suspect political geography, that James should be known as the King of England, the Italians refused to go along with the charade. They referred to James as the 'local king' or 'king here', to distinguish him from the Hanovarian 'king there'. Plots and pleas mingled with family disputes. Sincere Jacobites began to look to Charles Edward for leadership and when the final Jacobite challenge was made in 1745 it was the young prince who led it. His father slipped further into the background. One visitor felt that the quixotic Chevalier had begun to acquire the look of an idiot, and noted that he spent an increasing amount of his time in ponderous and introverted prayer. When the death was announced of the self-styled James VIII — hardly less of a nickname that any of the others he attracted during the course of his miserable life — the news drew scarcely a ripple of comment from the courts and council chambers of Europe. This unmourned departure was not what James would have wanted, although it was probably just what he would have predicted.

'CHARLES III'
Pretender to the throne 1766-1788

Born: 1720. Died: 1788. Marriage: Princess Louisa of Stolberg. No children.

It would have been strange if Scotland had lost her independence without throwing up some sort of romantic nationalist hero. The figure who eventually emerged in this role, several decades after the union, was Bonnie Prince Charlie, the elder son of 'James VIII' and Maria Sobieska. As well as the rather dashing epithet which he acquired in popular mythology, he was also known as the 'Young Pretender' and the 'Young Chevalier', variations of his father's nicknames.

Uncritically lauded by Jacobite Scots (especially when in their cups) and by purveyors of imaginative fiction, he has been treated with equally unjustified scorn by some professional historians, who cannot find a good word to say for him. In fact Charles Edward was little different from any other human being, a complex and sometimes conflicting knot of characteristics. Given a reasonably stable upbringing, he would probably have made a competent constitutional monarch. As it was, he inherited not a crown but a cause, and a pretty hopeless one at that. It would have taken a man of exceptional talent, assisted by more than a modicum of luck, to make anything of this inheritance. Charles was not so blessed.

Superficially at least the Young Pretender contrasted favourably with the Old. He was good looking and much more animated in expression than his father. His large blue eyes, set in a pale face above a generous mouth, won him great favour among the swarthy Italians, who have always had a soft spot for pretty children. Although lean, he was physically tough and quite sporty, being a competent golfer and good shot. As befitted one raised among the treasures of the renaissance he showed good taste and some musical ability. At 17 a truncated grand tour completed a haphazard education at the hands of Protestants, Jesuits and Jacobites, leaving him with a catholic but unfocused knowledge of eighteenth-century Europe and its affairs. He spoke Italian, French, English and Spanish, and later quickly picked up sufficient Gaelic to make himself understood. We can only guess at the effect the unpleasant bickering of his parents had on him.

Whereas in the early years of the century it was the Spanish succession which had drawn the European powers into conflict with each other, in the 1740s it was the fate of Austria which divided them. As far as Britain and France were concerned the conflict was also a maritime and colonial one. In these circumstances it was inevitable that Louis XV (the great-grandson of Louis XIV) should look at his hand to see what it held. The Jacobite card, although by no means a trump by this time, remained at his disposal and was a useful one to play. Toasts to the uninspiring 'king over the water' were still being drunk by disaffected politicians in England and Scotland, and when war broke out in 1739 a fairly vigorous Jacobite Association was formed.

The plan concocted by the Jacobites and their hesitant French paymasters was for the Young Pretender to land in Scotland in 1744 with a force of 10,000 regular troops and plenty of money and arms. The soldiers assembled at Dunkirk and set sail under the command of Marshal Saxe. Charles had said farewell to his father in Rome, promising to return either in a coffin or bearing three crowns. (In the event he neither won the latter nor ended up in the former. And he did not return home for a long time.) Having crossed Europe in disguise, as his father had done before him, the dashing figurehead joined the invasion fleet. Once again, however, the weather intervened to thwart the Jacobites and the ships were forced by storms to return to port. The French now prevaricated, unwilling to risk further humiliation. So Charles, young and irrepressibly optimistic, decided to go it alone. His invasion would take place, he swore, even if he had only 'a single footman' with him. He pawned his mother's rubies to raise money and ignoring all cautious advice he set out from Nantes in June 1745 with 700 soldiers in two ships. Before he reached Scotland he had lost one of the vessels, forced to return by the bombardment of an English warship. When he landed at Eriskay in the Outer Hebrides he was accompanied by only seven companions. It was about time the luck of the Stewarts changed.

Bonnie Prince Charlie's adventure had no backing from continental Jacobites: he had not told the French government or his father what he intended. His war chest amounted to 4000 gold French coins. It was indeed a rash venture. Yet for a few months it seemed, against all the odds, as if it might succeed. Unlike his father, grandfather and great-grandfather Charles had the ability to inspire devotion. He was a fine talker, too. When he set foot on Scottish soil the local chiefs advised him to return home. He retorted with instinctive theatricality, but less accuracy, that he had come home. Later, as Donald Cameron of Lochiel was hesitating about whether to side with the rebels or not, the prince goaded him to his side with the retort: 'Lochiel may stay at home and learn from the newspapers the fate of his Prince.'

Charles' confidence was infectious and before long a considerable force had assembled, mainly from the central and western Highlands, and the north-east Lowlands. A few clan chiefs refused his summons, mainly on the grounds that he had not brought the promised 10,000 regular troops which were considered necessary for the venture to have any chance of success. Presbyterians also shunned his ranks. The most important catch was Lord George Murray, a commander of remarkable brilliance. Charles' only military experience prior to 1745 had been when at the age of 13 he had attended the six

Prince Charles Edward Stuart painted by H. D. Hamilton in about 1785. No longer Bonnie (as this portrait shows) and a confirmed alcoholic, 'Charles III' drifted around Europe with increasingly aimlessness after his defeat in 1746. He had returned to the continent a hero, but the celebrity was more than his vain personality could stand and he descended into a life of debauchery, finally dying in Rome in 1788.

day seige of Gaeta in Italy. He had landed in Scotland on 25th July. He raised his standard at Glenfinnan less than a month later, was in Perth by 4th September and Edinburgh a fortnight after that. On 21st September a small force of Hanovarian regulars under the command of Sir John Cope was routed at Prestonpans. In London there was genuine consternation as Charles set himself up in Holyrood palace. But it was one thing to use the ferocity and loyalty of untrained Highlanders to seize north and east Scotland, quite another to take over the whole government of Britain. Against the advice of Murray, Charles decided to press on. Relations between the two men had become strained, the prince resenting the tactlessly expressed realism of the older man and jealous of his military talent, and Lord George irritated by Charles' enthusiastic optimism. At one point, after the fall of Carlisle in November, the rash Young Pretender went as far as telling Murray he was dismissed, only to find himself forced to revoke the decision when the Highland chiefs refused to serve under anyone else.

From a military point of view the descent into England was a brilliant exercise and by December the Jacobite army had reached Derby unchallenged. The march was also successful as a piece of propaganda; the Highland irregulars were well-ordered and the courts of Europe stood agog as news of the extraordinary progress filtered through. But as a recruiting drive the mission was a failure. Only a handful of supporters joined the prince's ranks while those of George II's generals grew all the time. On Friday 4th December — 'Black Friday' — Charles grumpily agreed to retire. He had no choice. Murray and the chiefs would not proceed deeper into what they saw as a certain trap, and the men would take orders from no-one but them. The army moved back to Scotland in good order. In mid-January they skillfully won another fight with the Hanovarian regulars, this time at Falkirk. It was clear that the Jacobite beast still had fight left in it. The shadowing force of the Duke of Cumberland, King George's third son, kept their distance as the prince's tired and diminishing army made its way north to Inverness. Here Charles established his headquarters. Murray wished to retire into the mountains where the Highlanders could be used to their best advantage in guerilla warfare. Charles and his band of Irish favourites would not agree. The thought of living rough did not appeal to them (although Charles was soon to have more experience of this than he bargained for). Besides, Charles was a man of gestures. He wanted a battle, a sweeping Jacobite victory. Once more Murray's wise advice was rejected, and Charles had his battle.

What took place on Culloden Moor on 16th April 1746 was in fact more of a slaughter than a battle. The Jacobite troops were exhausted and ill-equipped to meet Cumberland's regulars. At least a fifth of the Jacobites were too ill to fight and their ammunition was the wrong calibre for their cannon. Moreover, the men of the hillsides were asked to charge over open ground against grape shot and well-aimed musket fire. The result was horrible butchery. The spell of the Bonnie Prince over his men was finally broken. 'There you go for a damned

Flora Macdonald risked her life in helping Prince Charles escape after the defeat of the Jacobites by 'Butcher' Cumberland. She was arrested and taken to London but such was her fame by this time that the authorities soon released her. She later married and emigrated to America for a few years. This portrait by Richard Wilson shows a rather demure young lady, not at all the romantic heroine of subsequent legend.

cowardly Italian!' shouted one of Charles' men after the prince as he fled from the battlefield.

The Battle of Culloden marked the end of the Jacobite cause and the close of a long chapter in Highland history. Cumberland the 'butcher' pursued Jacobites and their sympathisers with ruthless cruelty. Hundreds died, many more were deported. Steps were taken to ensure that the Highlands could never again provide an invader with a ready-made army. The area was heavily garrisoned. Traditional loyalties were ended with the abolition of hereditable jurisdictions and military land tenures, and through the forfeiture of estates. The Gaelic language and Highland dress were outlawed. If the prosperity of the Highlands was not yet broken, its spirit certainly was.

For the five months between the time he ran from Culloden Moor and the moment he was picked up at Arisaig by a French ship in late September, Charles was a hunted man. More than anything else it was the storybook adventures of this period which were responsible for the legend which grew up around him, and which eventually destroyed him. A reward of £30,000 was put on his head, a sum which represented far more to an eighteenth-century Highlander than does the largest pools win to a present-day crofter. Charles slept in the open, and smoked and drank with the men who sheltered him. In fact he developed quite a taste for drink, a habit that was to stay with him for the rest of his life. He adopted disguises and travelled miles on foot over rugged terrain in inclement weather, all the time promising that those who helped him would be handsomely rewarded. As it turned out not even Flora MacDonald, who was arrested and taken to London for sheltering Charles as her maid 'Betty Burke', received a farthing.

Bonnie Prince Charlie returned to the continent a folk hero. His adventures were told and retold, each time with new romantic embellishments or glosses on the prince's courage and daring. Already a spoilt and vain man, the adulation was fatal. He split with his father over the elevation of his brother Henry to the rank of cardinal, and with Louis XV over the terms for French support for a new Jacobite expedition. When Britain and France made peace at Aix-la-Chapelle in 1748 the parties agreed that Charles should leave French soil. He petulantly refused to do so and had to be seized and moved to Avignon by force. He then disappeared with his mistress, Clementina Walkenshaw, whom he had met in Scotland after the retreat from Derby. By now his good looks were deserting him and he was acquiring an unsavoury reputation as a drunkard. In 1750 he visited London in disguise and became a member of the Church of England in order to make himself more acceptable to the English, though it can have done little to endear him to the Scots. Unwilling to forfeit continental Catholic support, however, he kept the conversion secret, thus making it pretty pointless. He may also have visited southern England in disguise on more than one other occasion.

Clementina left Charles in 1760, tired of his debauchery and feckless boasting. She took their daughter, Charlotte with her. The Young Pretender returned to Rome after his father's death in 1766. He adopted the title 'Charles III' and was welcomed by the Pope, although he never formally recognised the Pretender's title. But the Young Chevalier's cause and his personality were now both beyond repair. Recollecting some befuddled sense of duty to perpetuate the Stewart line, and encouraged by the prospect of a French pension, in 1772 he married Louisa of Stolberg, bestowing upon her the title Countess of Albany. The union was short, unhappy and barren. By 1780 the Countess was living in Rome with her lover.

Like a pointed Victorian morality tale on the evils of alcohol, the story of the Young Pretender included a sentimental little chapter at its end. Deserted and unloved, in his sodden loneliness the exile sent for his daughter, Charlotte, of whom he was genuinely fond. Surprisingly, she obeyed his summons and brought him a little temporary happiness. She even managed to persuade him to dry out for a while. But Charles was not a strong character and he was too depressed for the reformation to last. He returned to his old ways and died at the age of 67 on 31st January 1788, almost exactly 99 years since his grandfather had been driven from his throne.

HENRY BENEDICT STUART ('HENRY IX' 1788-1807)

Born: 1725. Died: 1807. Unmarried.

Henry Benedict Maria Clement Stuart was the second son of the Old Pretender. He was born in Rome and although he is said to have visited his brother's forces at Dunkirk as they prepared for their assault on Scotland in 1744, his prime interest remained the work of the Roman Catholic church in the Mediterranean world. His life, therefore, is really just a postscript to the history of the Jacobite movement. He showed little or no knowledge of Scottish affairs and never set foot in any corner of the British Isles.

Clearly influenced by his deeply religious mother, Henry became a Roman Catholic at an early age. He rose rapidly in the hierarchy of the church. His royal blood must have helped him in his career but he also was a man of ability. He looked rather like his father, though contemporaries said that he was more spirited than either of the Pretenders, and those who met him were attracted by his genial demeanour. He was also tactful, as befitted a leading member of the Catholic hierarchy. His first major appointment was as Bishop of Frascati, the area just south of Rome celebrated for its refreshing white wine. Here Henry established his primary residence. He went on to become a cardinal in 1747, an appointment which separated him from his brother and certainly

Although from time to time various Jacobite pretenders of German descent have appeared since 1807, Henry Benedict Stuart (1725-1807) was the last direct descendant of James VII. He showed little interest in his supposed right to the throne of the United Kingdom and concentrated on his career in the Roman Catholic church. This portrait by H. D. Hamilton shows him in the robes of a cardinal, a position he achieved in 1747.

put paid to any slight hope he might have harboured of ever being favourably received in either England or Scotland. He later became an archbishop and acquired valuable benefices in France. Also in receipt of a generous Spanish pension, by the age of 40 he was a very wealthy man.

Jacobitism is best described as Henry's hobby. As a cardinal he is reported to have worn ermine as a mark of his royalty and he was sometimes known as the Cardinal of York, as he had been given the title Duke of York as a child. He does not seem to have cared for the equivalent Scots accolade, Duke of Albany. He showed a similar disregard for Scottish sensibilities in 1788 when he proclaimed himself 'Henry IX' on the death of his brother. His correct appellation in Scotland should have been Henry I. At no time did he ever press his dynastic claims or cause the British authorities any nuisance. Later when he fell on hard times this was to stand him in good stead. The cardinal's relations with his brother were never affectionate. The exalted cleric was probably embarrassed by the Young Pretender's excesses and unsavoury reputation. But Henry was no prude. When the Countess of Albany left her husband in 1777 Henry found a place for her in his house in Rome and was sufficiently broad minded to permit her lover, Alfieri, to pay court to her there.

The arrival of the French Revolution brought a sharp reverse in the fortunes of the cardinal-king. He lost the income of his French livings and had his Spanish pension stopped. Nevertheless, he was still well enough off to contribute generously to the tribute demanded of Pope Pius VI by Napoleon. Henry handed over many of the remaining Stewart family jewels, including a ruby which was said to have been worth the remarkable sum of £50,000. In 1799, however, French troops sacked Henry's house in Frascati, causing the cardinal to lose all he possessed. He was fortunate to escape with his life. The ill-luck of the Stewarts/Stuarts had persisted to the end.

The final years of the last Stuart witnessed at last a reconciliation between the Hanovarians and the dynasty they had supplanted. As the destitute cleric wandered round Italy, help arrived from a surprising source. George III, hearing of the cardinal's misfortune and recognising a fellow enemy of revolutionary excesses, sent Henry a present of £2000. It was received with much gratitude. The ageing bachelor now retired to Frascati, where he died in July 1807. In his will he reciprocated George's kindness by leaving the crown jewels, which James VII had taken with him into exile in 1688, to the Prince of Wales, the future George IV. With this gesture the Jacobite charade was finally over.

THE MONARCHY SINCE THE UNION

A specifically Scottish monarchy ceased to exist in 1707. For a long time before that the institution had become anglicised, so when the change came it had little effect in Scotland. James VI had returned to his native country only once after setting himself up in England in 1603. His son Charles I made two formal visits to his northern kingdom, both unsatisfactorily provocative. His son used Scotland as a springboard for an invasion of England in 1650 but did not return after his restoration 10 years later. Discounting the Pretenders, he was the last reigning monarch to set foot in Scotland for more than 150 years. James VII and Anne made brief visits north before they came into their inheritance but never thereafter. The country might as well have been a republic for all it saw of its crowned heads.

The Hanovarians, who acquired the British crown in 1714, had no especial dislike of Scotland; they just felt no particular compunction to visit it. To begin with at least they were as alien to the English as to the Scots. In the pre-Romantic era Scotland's wildernesses and relatively inclement weather held no attraction for visitors and the first three Georges were subjected to a continual barrage of disparaging anti-Scottish prejudice from their English courtiers. In fact George I took some personal interest in Scottish affairs, closely following the progress of the Act of Union and insisting that £20,000 from the estates of the Jacobites who had rebelled in 1715 be spent on public schools in the Highlands. However, reconciliation did not really come about until the early nineteenth century.

In 1819 the Prince Regent donated £50 towards the monument to the exiled House of Stewart being set up in Rome. In doing this he showed the same lack of vindictiveness as his father had done when he generously gave a pension to the impoverished 'Henry IX'. The Prince, now George IV, took his reconciliation with the Scottish nation a step further in 1822 when he made a state visit to Scotland. It was done with great ceremony (stage-managed by Walter Scott) and the king tried hard to play his part as tactfully as possible. He wrapped himself in a gigantic kilt, carefully cut to accommodate his impressive bulk, and spoke with endearing but inaccurate familiarity of clans, tartans and chiefs. He resided at Holyrood Palace, made startling appearances in the Royal Stewart plaid and full Highland regalia, and thoroughly enjoyed himself. But it was his niece Victoria who really made Scotland her own.

On Victoria's first visit to Edinburgh the government feared for her life, and it was discovered that the draughty and dilapidated Holyrood was no longer a fitting residence for a monarch used to modern comforts. It is not surprising to learn, therefore, that the queen was not immediately enamoured of Scotland. But it did not take her long to discover there the peace that she always lacked in the south. Soon she was speaking of the 'dear, dear highlands', climbing mountains on a shaggy pony, attending the kirk's services, dressing the peasants in kilts and acquiring a little place of her own, Balmoral Castle. Her German husband, Albert, was forced into a kilt of his own and sent out into the dripping glens on hunting trips. After Albert's death Victoria visited Balmoral more frequently and, travelling about incognito, came to know well the ordinary people of the Highlands whom she found invariably honest, sharp and kindly. The Prince of Wales received some of his school and university education in Edinburgh. Thus was the long-broken link between the royal family and Scotland securely and lovingly reforged.

Since the time of Victoria the British royal family have been careful to maintain their close ties with Scotland. But this has been not so much a matter of duty as of delight. The Scottish moors afford a wonderful escape from the cloying sophistication of the south and provide fine sport for those who like shooting or less martial outdoor pursuits. Balmoral remains the family's summer residence. Here they gather to recuperate from the endless round of formal engagements which dominate the rest of the year. Prince Charles, whose penchant for quiet places is well known, has a particular fondness for Scotland. He was educated at Gordonstoun School in Moray, has written about Scotland and retires on occasion to remote areas to recharge his intellectual and spiritual batteries. However, the closest link between the royal family and Scotland has come about through marriage.

The Lyon family can trace their ancestry back to the time of Robert the Bruce, from whom they are descended. In the fourteenth century they became barons of Glamis. Later the family acquired the title Earl of Strathmore and Kinghorne, and married into the Bowes family, a union which gave rise to their present surname, Bowes-Lyon. There are few more distinguished ancient Scottish families. In 1923 Albert Duke of York married the lovely Lady Elizabeth Angela Marguerite Bowes-Lyon, third daughter of the fourteenth earl. When his brother, Edward VIII, abdicated in 1936 Albert became King George VI and his Scottish wife Queen Consort. Both as queen and Queen Mother (a title she adopted after her husband's death) Elizabeth has captivated the hearts of the entire nation, and her winning blend of grace, intelligence and spontaneity ensure that wherever she goes this most charming of Scottish ladies is her nation's finest ambassador. Her childhood was spent at Glamis castle and she still spends a considerable part of her time in her native land.

Today, although the functions of the monarchy are purely symbolic and ceremonial, they are nevertheless vitally important. They provide the nation with a non-political focal point, a symbol of its unity. The ancient monarchs of Scotland devoted their lives to the creation and preservation of a nation. Our present royal family may have broader responsibilities and different means but its ultimate task is much the same. In every way it has proved worthy of its distinguished heritage.

Map 4
THE CLANS OF SCOTLAND

Pentland Firth

SINCLAIR

MACKAY GUNN

MACLEOD

Stornoway

Lewis

SUTHERLAND

MACLEOD

R O S S

Dunrobin

MACDONELL

Moray Firth

MUNRO

M A C L E O D

North Uist

Dunvegan
MACLEOD
Skye

MACKENZIE

Elgin
ROSE   DUNBAR

INNES

FORBES *Peterhead*
KEITH

FRASER

Inverness

MACKINNON

CLAN
DONALD

CHISHOLM

GRANT

MACINTOSH

Spey

GRANT

G O R D O N

FORBES
Aberdeen

M A C D O N A L D

South Uist

MACDONELL

Grant
Fort Augustus

MACPHERSON

Braemar

Dee

KEITH

MACNEIL
Barra

Rhum

M A C D O N A L D

STEWART

FARQUHARSON

LINDSAY

CAMERON

MENZIES

Blair Atholl

OGILVY

Montrose

M A C L E A N

Coll

Tiree

MACLEAN

MACQUARRIE

Mull

Iona

Fort William

STEWART

MACLEAN

C A M P B E L L

Oban

MACGREGOR

Inverary

CAMPBELL

ROBERTSON

M U R R A Y

RUTHVEN

MACNAB

DRUMMOND

LYON

Perth

MONCRIEF

CARNEGIE

Dundee

Firth of Tay

St. Andrews

LINDSAY

Jura

CLAN
DONALD
Islay

MACLACHLAN

LAMONT

STUART

Rothesay

S T E W A R T

Loch Lomond

GRAHAM *Stirling*

HAMILTON

Firth of Forth

HAMILTON

Glasgow

Edinburgh

LINDSAY

HOME

Berwick

MACALISTER

HAMILTON
Arran

MONTGOMERIE

Firth of Clyde

Ayr

C L A N   D O N A L D

DUNBAR

Clyde

D O U G L A S

H A Y

Tweed

Kelso

KERR

SCOTT

DOUGLAS

KENNEDY

STEWART

JOHNSTON

Dumfries

Castle Douglas

Carlisle

0   25 miles

Solway Firth

IRELAND

THE MONARCHS AND THE CLANS

The word 'clan' comes from the Gaelic for 'family' or 'children'. In early Scotland the family was the basic unit of political cohesion, demanding loyalty over any larger grouping. The head of the family was the chief and he designated his successor not through primogeniture but by the system of tanistry. Clans were originally a feature of all parts of Scotland, though the rugged and poor conditions of Highland living made the system stronger there than in the more fertile Lowlands. The early medieval Scottish monarchs sought to create a united kingdom in which their authority was universally recognised to be supreme. From the late eleventh century onwards efforts were made to introduce the feudal system. Since its premise was that all land was the king's and was held directly or indirectly from him in return for service, feudalism was the antithesis of the decentralised clan system. Much of subsequent Scottish domestic history is the story of successive kings struggling to exert their authority over the clan-centred remoter areas of the realm. Sometimes they met with notable success. On the other hand, during periods of weak central direction, local loyalties swiftly re-emerged. It was only when the English crushed the clans supporting the Jacobites in 1746 that their power was finally broken for good.

The great Scottish families were originally a cosmopolitan lot. The Gordons were of Norman descent, the Murrays were Flemings, the MacLeods were Norse and the most famous of all, the Stewarts, were originally from Brittany. Somerled, the twelfth century founder of the great clan of Donalds and MacDonalds, was the son-in-law of Olaf, King of Man. Each clan was tightly organised. Its chief was an immensely powerful figure, not just a military commander but a judge, arbiter, policy-maker and executive of undisputed authority. The surprising success of Bonnie Prince Charlie in raising a formidable fighting force in a few weeks in 1745 was due in no small part to the power of the clan chiefs who gave him their loyalty. A skillful monarch was able to persuade the Highlanders that he was their 'chief of chiefs'; even so, no clansmen would follow him unless led by their local chief. Beneath the chief in the hierarchy were the cadet branches of the clan, each headed by a chieftain. They in turn granted land on long-term leases or 'tacks' to tacksmen who could then sublet it to their tenants, the ordinary clansmen. A chief was honour-bound to avenge a member of his clan, however humble, who had suffered at the hands of a member of another group. This led to ghastly vendettas, marked by cruelty and treachery. The massacre at Glencoe (1692) is only the best known among hundreds of such outrages. The fact that it was perpetrated by the Campbells, the ambitious and forward-looking clan who had successfully challenged the power of the MacDonalds, gave condemnation of it a particularly vituperative edge.

One of the most extraordinary clan battles occurred in 1603. It was arranged by the Campbells, whose scheming chief, the Earl of Argyll, wished to see an end to the MacGregors. MacGregors and Colquhouns fought a pitched battle in Glenfruin before a gathering of ghoulish onlookers. Although outnumbered, the MacGregors won a remarkable victory, losing two of their men to the Colquhouns' 140. The Earl of Argyll had his way, however. Had he been hoping for a slaughter of the MacGregors, he was obviously disappointed. But now a furious and embarrassed James VI stepped in. For perpetrating such a blatant breach of the peace the entire MacGregor clan was outlawed and its name abolished. Somehow the 'nameless clan' survived proscription for 139 years. When it was finally reinstated in 1775 a total of 826 MacGregor clansmen revealed themselves. Such was the power of clan cohesion and loyalty.

Surnames were not used in the more remote areas of the Highlands until the eighteenth century. This made it almost impossible to tell from their name to which clan a person belonged. A man (James MacDonald, for example) was simply given a name (James) which was attached to that of his father (Donald) by the prefix 'mac' meaning 'son of'. The next generation became MacJames, and so on. When surnames were eventually adopted they were either borrowed from the chief (or a variation of his name), or taken from a man's employment, or the father's name then in use could simply be retained for future generations. To the uninitiated this produced a bewildering variety of names within a clan.

The use of the tartan has been noted as early as the thirteenth century. But not until the romantic revival of the nineteenth century did it become the exclusive badge of a clan. Before that each district wove its own pattern and Highlanders could be seen sporting with impunity a mixture of tartans. Many of the original patterns were lost when the wearing of tartan was outlawed between 1747 and 1782. Therefore most tartans we see today are of comparatively recent origin. It is very unlikely that the tartan had any function as a warrior's distinguishing mark, for clansmen removed their cumbersome plaids before fighting and patterns were too similar to be told apart at a distance or in poor light. To the terror or amusement of their foes, Highlanders usually charged into battle wearing only a shirt, and sometimes not even that. The kilt was not adopted until the seventeenth century, before which time Highlanders wrapped themselves in the 16ft x 5ft plaid or 'feileadh mor'.

The clans were a mixed blessing to those seeking to turn Scotland into a nation state. They made the enforcement of a uniform system of law very difficult and were the cause of innumerable outbreaks of disorder. Yet at times of national crisis they could usually be relied on to produce doughty if not always disciplined soldiers. In the end, however, it was this capacity which led to their downfall. In 1745 they rose to the call of a king for the last time. But their blind loyalty was misplaced and for the mistake they were so clipped that they could never rise again.

A BRIEF CHRONOLOGY OF THE PRINCIPAL EVENTS IN THE HISTORY OF SCOTLAND AND HER MONARCHY

BC

c 6000	Middle Stone Age; first settlers reach Scotland
c 4000	New Stone Age
c 1500	Skara Brae settlement founded
c 500	Iron-working Celts arrive in Scotland

AD

80	Romans under Agricola reach the Tay
c 123	Hadrian's Wall built
c 140	Antonine Wall built
c 400	St Ninian arrives in Scotland
c 500	Settlers from Ireland found Dalriada
c 550	Angles settle in south-east Scotland
563	St Columba founds monastery on Iona
794	First Viking raids
c 841-c 859	KENNETH I: HOUSE OF ALPIN
843	Union of Picts and Scots to form Alba
c 859-c 863	DONALD I
c 863-c 877	CONSTANTINE I
877-878	AED
878-c 889	GIRIC and EOCHAID
889-900	DONALD II
c 890	Earldom of Orkney founded by Vikings
900-943	CONSTANTINE II
943-954	MALCOLM I
954-962	INDULF
c 960	Indulf takes Edinburgh
962-c 967	DUBH
c 967-971	CULEN
971-995	KENNETH II
995-997	CONSTANTINE III
997-1005	KENNETH III
1005-1034	MALCOLM III
1018	Battle of Carham; Lothian annexed by Malcolm III
1034-1040	DUNCAN I: HOUSE OF DUNKELD
1043	Strathclyde annexed by Scottish kingdom
1040-1057	MACBETH
1057-1058	LULACH
1058-1093	MALCOLM III, 'Canmore'
1072	Malcolm III submits to William the Conqueror
1093-1097	DONALD III, 'Donald Ban' (deposed for a while in 1094)

1094	DUNCAN II
1097-1107	EDGAR
1098	Magnus Barelegs of Norway takes Western Isles
1107-1124	ALEXANDER I
1124-1153	DAVID I
1138	Scots defeated at the Battle of the Standard
1139	Earl Henry given Northumbria by King Stephen
1153-1165	MALCOLM IV
1154	Henry I of England takes back gains of David I
1165-1214	WILLIAM I, 'the Lion'
1175	Treaty of Falaise: William I recognises Henry II as his feudal lord
1189	Quit-claim of Canterbury reverses Treaty of Falaise: Scotland recovers her independence
1192	Scottish church declared to be under direct papal control
1214-1249	ALEXANDER II
1237	Treaty of York establishes Tweed-Solway line as boundary between Scotland and England
1249-1286	ALEXANDER III
1263	Battle of Largs
1266	Treaty of Perth cedes Western Isles to Scotland
1286-1290	MARGARET
1290-1292	INTERREGNUM: the 'Great Cause'
1292-1296	JOHN: HOUSE OF BALLIOL. Scotland's independence threatened
1295	Alliance with France
1296	Scots defeated at Battle of Dunbar; John deprived of his throne
1296-1306	INTERREGNUM
1297	Rising of William Wallace
1305	Wallace captured and executed
1306-1329	ROBERT I, 'the Bruce': HOUSE OF BRUCE
1314	English defeated at Bannockburn
1320	Declaration of Arbroath sets out Scottish independence
1328	Treaty of Edinburgh-Northampton confirms independence
1329-1371	DAVID II
1332	Forces of David II defeated by Edward Balliol
1333	David II sent to France for safety
1341	David II returns to Scotland
1346	David II captured at Battle of Neville's Cross
1357	Treaty of Berwick releases David II
1371-1390	ROBERT II: HOUSE OF STEWART
1390-1406	ROBERT III
1406	Prince James captured by English while making his way to France
1406-1437	JAMES I
1406	Robert Duke of Albany acts as Governor for James
1412	University of St Andrews founded

1420	Albany dies, succeeded by his son Murdoch
1424	Return of James I
1426	Foundation of the court known later as the 'Session'
1437-1460	JAMES II
1440	'Black Dinner' murder of the Douglases
1451	University of Glasgow founded
1455	Douglases defeated at the Battle of Arkinholm
1460-1488	JAMES III
1466	King James seized by the Boyds
1468-1472	Scotland acquires the Orkney and Shetland Isles
1472	Supremacy of the see of St Andrews recognised
1482	Baronial revolt at Lauder Bridge
1488-1513	JAMES IV, 'James of the Iron Belt'
1493	Lordship of the Isles to the crown
1495	University founded at Aberdeen
1496	Education Act. James IV backs the pretender Perkin Warbeck
1505-6	Foundation of Royal College of Surgeons
1513	Battle of Flodden
1513-1542	JAMES V
1528	James V seizes power. First Scottish Protestant martyr
1532	College of Justice established
1542	Scots defeated at Solway Moss
1542-1567	MARY I
1544-5	'Rough Wooing' of Henry VIII's troops
1547	Scots victory at Pinkie
1548	Queen Mary to France
1554	Mary of Guise proclaimed Regent
1560	Protestant rebellion
1561	Queen Mary returns to Scotland
1566	Murder of Rizzio
1567	Murder of Darnley. Queen Mary deposed
1567-1625	JAMES VI
1568	Mary flees into England
1578	Second Book of Discipline issued
1582	King James seized in the 'Raid of Ruthven'
1583	University of Edinburgh founded
1586	Formal accord between James and Elizabeth I of England
1587	Mary 'Queen of Scots' executed
1592	Authorisation of Presbyterian church government
1603	Death of Queen Elizabeth I of England
	James VI succeeds to the English throne: HOUSE OF STUART
1607	Union between Scotland and England rejected by English
1610	Episcopal authority restored
1616	Education Act

1618	'Five Articles of Perth'
1625-1649	CHARLES I
1625	Act of Revocation passed
1633	Charles I visits Scotland
1637	New Prayer Book introduced into Scotland, provoking rebellion
1638	National Covenant launched
1643	Solemn League and Covenant between English parliament and Scots, who then enter English Civil War
1645	Defeat of Montrose
1646	Charles I surrenders to Scots
1647	'Engagement' signed between Charles I and Covenanters
1649	Execution of Charles I by English
1649-1685	CHARLES II
1651	Charles II crowned at Scone, defeated at Worcester by Oliver Cromwell and goes into exile. English troops occupy Scotland. English and Scottish governments united
1660	Restoration of Charles II
1666	Rebellion of Covenanters
1679	Murder of Archbishop Sharp. Covenanters' rebellion defeated
1685-1689	JAMES VII
1686	Catholics granted freedom of worship by royal prerogative
1688	James VII driven from England
1689-1702	WILLIAM II and MARY II
1689-1690	Revolution Settlement: Scotland Presbyterian again
1692	Massacre of Glencoe
1694	Death of Queen Mary
1695	Bank of Scotland founded
1698-1700	Darien Scheme
1701	Death of the exiled James VII; Jacobites proclaim 'James VIII'
1702-1714	ANNE
1704	Act of Security
1707	Union of Scotland with England
1708	Jacobite rebellion
1714-1727	GEORGE I: HOUSE OF HANOVER
1715	Jacobite rebellion
1719	Jacobite rebellion
1727-1760	GEORGE II
1736	Porteous riots
1745-6	Last Jacobite rebellion ends with Battle of Culloden
1760-1820	GEORGE III
1766	Death of 'James VIII'; Jacobites proclaim 'Charles III'
1788	Death of 'Charles III'
1807	Death of 'Henry IX'; the Jacobite threat is extinguished
1822	George IV visits Scotland

INDEX

Stewart → Stuart in 1603 (see p. 116)